THE BLUE ANGEL

The life and films of Marlene Dietrich

by

David Stuart Ryan

The Blue Angel – the life and films of Marlene Dietrich
David Stuart Ryan
Copyright 2013 by David Stuart Ryan

Kozmik Press

London and Washington DC

ISBN-13: 978-1456465780
ISBN-10: 1456465783
BISAC: Biography & Autobiography / Entertainment &
Performing Arts

David Stuart Ryan

More information about this book and other Kozmik Press titles at http://www.kozmikhoroscopes.com/kozmik.htm

Also at amazon.com, amazon.co.uk

About the author

David Stuart Ryan was born in 1943 at Kingston upon Thames, Surrey, England. He was educated at Wimbledon College and King's College London where he read Ancient History and Philosophy as well as editing the London University newspaper, *Sennet*.

After working as an advertising copywriter he set off on a round the world journey that took some 6 years to complete, visiting Europe, India, SE Asia, Australia, Fiji and America.

Some of the background to this book comes from his living and working in the Netherlands and Germany. This was supplemented with research interviewing people who knew Marlene well, such as Burt Bacharach, her musical collaborator in her stage shows, and Bernard Hall, her assistant for many years. He was also in touch with Leni Riefenstahl and Billy Wilder, who was resident in Berlin at the time of *The Blue Angel* being made working as a scriptwriter. In fact, the plot of his greatest film, *Some Like It Hot* draws on a similar story set in Berlin in the time of the Jazz Age.

Other books by the author

Novels

The Affair is All
Looking for Kathmandu
Taboo
The Lost Journal of Robyn Hood – Outlaw
1967

Biography

John Lennon's Secret

Poetry

The Sphere of the Moon Goddess
The Conjunction of the Sun and Moon
Postcards From Around the Globe
New New World – the Land of Australia
and the Islands of Fiji
Home – and a Journey to the USA

Travel

India – a Guide to the Experience
America – a Guide to the Experience

All these titles are available through Amazon and other online
retailers such as Apple, Smashwords and Barnes and Noble.
This book is available in ebook and printed format from
Amazon and other booksellers.

Kozmik Press   London and Washington DC
www.kozmikhoroscopes.com/kozmik.htm

David Stuart Ryan

The story of Marlene Dietrich's life is the story of the 20th century.

Author David Stuart Ryan who wrote the bestselling biography 'John Lennon's Secret' explores the amazing and circuitous route that took her to Hollywood and riches.

But to understand the essential Marlene it is necessary to go right back in time to the era of *La Belle Époque* when a very feudal and settled order still existed in Europe.

'The Blue Angel' transports you to a glittering world that is all about to disappear in the maelstrom of world war. What emerges from the conflict is a feverish gaiety that seeks to put behind it all the suffering that has taken place.

You are entering the Jazz Age and a Berlin that having suffered hyperinflation decides anything goes. The Berliner Luft - the Berlin air - is what the locals call it.

This madcap atmosphere was to be recreated by a young journalist - Billy Wilder - when he made the journey to Hollywood. Indeed, the plot for his greatest film, 'Some Like It Hot', drew on his experiences in Berlin, and Billy Wilder was one of the respondents to the author when he came to write Marlene's story.

Marlene's big break came when she played a vampish nightclub singer of dubious morals, not a million miles away from her own background trying to survive in a world turned upside down.

The Blue Angel took her to America and a carefully constructed film star image which embodies all the dazzling wealth and influence of Hollywood at its most powerful and hypnotic.

Yet the more you get into the life of Marlene Dietrich, the greater the mystery becomes. Who was she really?

Only now can the expert analysis of David Stuart Ryan reveal the true Marlene Dietrich, the person behind the image, the human being behind the facade.

Was she indeed the blue angel?

Introduction

It should not have surprised the world so much that Maria Magdalene Dietrich decided to be buried in Berlin, alongside her mother Wilhelmine. Even though it was 60 years since she had left the city of her birth, it retained its pull on her heart, it was where she spent a too brief idyll in her youth before the world began crashing down around a shattered German nation.

In her last days the dying actress had the opportunity to look back across the chasm of the years, and came to realise that acceptance by her native city was what she had been searching for all those years away, and yet she would not have done anything different, given the awful circumstances.
For her, Berlin was epitomised by the beautiful Unter der Linden, with its great lime trees, and her mother's family jewellery shop on this fashionable thoroughfare at the peak of Germany's prosperity - before war was declared. This Berlin of her earliest memories was a fun-loving city, devoted to the arts of good living. German appreciation of high culture was one of the distinguishing marks of a civilisation that prided itself on its intellectual stature.

It was her grandmother who introduced her to an appreciation of the best of style and sophistication. She wore the furs and fabrics, jewels and perfumes that beguiled Marlene and, through the intermediary of the granddaughter, the whole world in the depths of the Depression.

Marlene Dietrich's early memories were of the smell of her Papa's beautiful shone leather boots, the sound of the smart click of his heels upon entering a room, the vision of him as an upright military man. He was the personification of the old Germany, the Germany that disappeared so soon after she had made its acquaintance in the days of her girlhood.

Doomed to be remembered as The Blue Angel, she was in reality one who had seen paradise very briefly and then experienced a fall from grace. She was to become a lamp in a darkened world, hardly in control of her life yet aware she had a destiny to fulfil. As you read the facts of her life, it is up to you, the understanding reader, to put your interpretation upon them.

It is an exotic journey retracing the passage a person has taken through all the events and people who make up a life. And for reasons we can only guess at, these events forced Marlene Dietrich on centre stage for much of the century. Experiencing all its sadness along with its too brief pleasures.

Love came to call, and departed as often. First her beloved father when she was not yet six years old, a void that she perhaps sought ever afterwards to fill. Yet that was only the first of the disappointments that attended on her career and path through life.

Even this fact of early loss is clouded in some murky ambivalence. For her father had already departed the family home to seek female consolation elsewhere before he died in Marlene's sixth year.

In a very special way, Berlin became like a parent to her after that aching loss. It was a place where she felt utterly at home, even or especially in its intimate clubs and restaurants, its theatres and amusement parks, its wide streets and its numerous secret cellars. The whole great pulsating city was hers to explore in a youth that had lost all guiding stars, where every day had to be lived on its own terms, for few knew what the next day would bring.

Ruin, love, rejection, advancement, violence, murder, happiness, laughter, wild abandon and an underlying restraint, Berlin provided all this in a day or even less. It was the centre of the artistic world, the city's theatre and film productions rivalled those of America and outshone the rest of Europe, in spite of all the chaos - perhaps because of it.

Der Berliner Luft it was called - 'The Berlin Air' where the mood was 'anything goes'. Imagine the scene for yourself. After the end of the Kaiser's War, the old Prussian Junker values of imperial Berlin were rejected. But the people simply abandoned these codes of behaviour, or as many of these as they wished, without putting much in their place. Art and experimentation were the order of the day, in the people's personal as much as their professional lives. The value of money collapsed, getting through the day on your wits was all that could be hoped for. Yet this could provide a heady excitement as the new worlds of the artists' imaginations tantalised with a seductive air.

Marlene sought to become a beckoning figure on the stage of life, a release to troubled mankind from its woes and cares, if only briefly. To dally in the Berlin of the 1920s was to see life in all its infinite variety. Men who felt unmanned by the war dressed as women, women lacking strong shoulders to lean on were forced back upon themselves to search for the hard masculine drive towards fulfilment or found it in strong women, still others were in an indeterminate no man's land between the two sexes. All was mixed and confused. Any new philosophy was seized upon and lived out to the full. To Marlene it was the heady breeze of freedom. The only demand was to follow your own star, and take it where it might lead.

It was a philosophy that only required she play herself, while others looked on and secretly approved. Could they know that The Blue Angel was playing herself? That she sought to know and consume their very souls, an experience she would survive, even if they were forever more touched and changed by this encounter, like moths singed by the candle flame?

After Berlin there were the mad excesses of America's Hollywood. It is an irony that an Austrian Jew, Jonas Sternberg, should introduce the wild ways of Berlin to a Depression-wracked America. But both he and Marlene had already lived right on the edge before the Depression struck.

For an America where nearly a quarter of the population had no job, no money, no prospects, only dreams to get them through each day, the unlikely pair of director and star created a furtive world of man and woman pursuing each other through an unearthly landscape where limits had dissolved and desires were fulfilled. They wrote their sexual attraction on the screens of the world and the masses responded with the thrill of recognition as they saw their most secret fantasies lived out before their eyes.

Josef von Sternberg, as he reinvented himself, liked to claim that he had discovered Marlene. But, as you will find, that is far too simple an interpretation of the way they came together, two dream weavers in need of confirmation on the physical level of their yearnings. He had been abused from very early on in life, and ambiguously wished to enslave himself at the same time as he enslaved his audiences to his vision. While Marlene set out quite consciously to capture the world's imagination as woman, pure and simple. That she had survived on the streets of Berlin was proof of how the dictates of the heart rule the head for any person. It was knowledge she put to use, just like the blue angel.

When she entered a ruined Germany at the end of Hitler's war, it was some shock to be offered a coffee by a German mayor who appeared to welcome her apocalyptic entry into his battered and blitzed town of Aachen at the head of avenging armies.

'Why are you singling me out for this delicious coffee?' she asked, perplexed at his ready acceptance of her among the American troops.

'Because you are the blue angel,' he replied simply.

Marlene had finally come home.

Chapter One

The early years

Maria Magdalene Dietrich took her first male lover when she was 17, and her last when she was 63. Only half her life was spent in intimate knowledge of male attraction and yet it is inevitable that she should be remembered as a screen goddess of love. The truth is far more complex, indeed sexual allure relates to the whole person, it is the essence of something within, and it attracts with a power in exact proportion to its unknown quantity.

Her beginnings would appear to have marked her out for privileged participation in the social life of a nation reaching the height of its power. Europe dominated the world, and was still increasing this power as distant lands in Asia and Africa were annexed and added to the already long list of colonies. Germany came late to this struggle for worldwide leadership and domination, which is perhaps why the German nation eyed the territories of the East in Russia with some fascination. Maria's grandfather had been a colonel in the crack Prussian Uhlan regiment and had gained the Iron Cross in the war with France in 1870-71. Her father, too, was a military man who had resigned his commission when he married her mother in 1893 when she was 23. This in itself was an unusual act for a Prussian gentleman, for all marriages in the very regulated society in which he moved had to be approved by the commanding officer. The preferred alliances were with the aristocrats and military families who formed the backbone the Junker class, the Prussian rulers of the newly formed German federation that Bismarck brought together. The code of conduct respected duty and obligation, saw its long line of tradition stretching back to the Teutonic knights who had defended Prussia from the invading Mongol hordes of Genghis Khan. Discipline was recognised as the supreme virtue in maintaining cohesion and superiority over the foe.

Even though her father was lost to her when she was aged five and a half years in the summer of 1907, his approach to life stayed with her. The need to bring order and discipline into home life, and the duty to perform one's work to the utmost of one's ability were guiding principles for long afterwards. She devoted her energies to this task like him. Her work was to play a screen goddess, but it was work nonetheless and it was her way of creating a bulwark against the endless tides of love and loss in her life. Her memories of her father were able to leave her feeling unsettled and tearful in her eighties. Even when alive, he was a remote glorious presence, immaculately attired in his Royal Prussian Police uniform, a Lieutenant in charge of some 600 men. He had joined the police force after resigning his commission and advanced far within its very structured ranks.

Her mother was from a well established family, originally artisans from Swabia, who in the early 19th century had come to Berlin and set up a jewellery business which developed until they had a shop in one of Berlin's most fashionable thoroughfares, Unter den Linden, a broad boulevard which hosted magnificent hotels. Wilhelmine Elisabeth Josephine Felsing devoted herself to her family and home once she had married the handsome police officer in the Royal Prussian Police. There were appearances and rank to keep up, and the social milieu required that the family should dress immaculately while being seen in the finest restaurants and cafés that adorned the very centre of Berlin where they lived. The Dietrich family moved frequently. First to larger apartments to match her father's rank and standing, and then after his death, to smaller and smaller apartments as her mother's income drastically decreased. She had used much of her dowry in maintaining the Dietrichs' position in society even when her husband was alive, for in that splendid decade before war broke out, now nostalgically referred to as La Belle

Epoch, fashion and luxurious living reached undreamt of heights all over Europe, and none more so than in a Berlin, the capital of a Germany rapidly growing richer and more powerful than any of her European neighbours.

Maria's sister, Elisabeth, was a year and a half older, having been born in 1900 as the new century began, but they both made their appearance at the Viktoria Louise school for girls at the same time. Maria's own birth date was December 27, 1901, shortly after 9pm in the evening, making her a Capricorn sun, with moon in Leo and Virgo on her rising sign. Much later, she would ask an astrologer to read the chart of any friend who she thought would benefit from the ancient art. Then, she had little idea her horoscope depicted an actress who longs to lead her life on the stage of life. Her early years at school were marked by her being younger than anyone else in the class. This age gap disguised a natural aptitude for learning and isolated her from the other girls. Her family's fall from high social position was marked by an early awareness that many of her schoolgirl contemporaries were collected by splendid horses and carriages, whereas her mother collected the two girls on foot. She was already aware that much she valued in life was likely to be taken from her unless she took energetic steps to remedy the situation.

But it was a happy childhood, with long summer holidays in the countryside, and a spell in the town of Weimar when her mother remarried in 1911, some four years after her father's death. She again had a military father, Colonel von Losch, but there was little time to get know this new man in her life before he was also taken from the family by the war which broke out in 1914, even before this he was often away on manoeuvres as the German army prepared for what it saw as an inevitable battle with Russia and France. The power of Russia, in particular, threatened the country's great wealth and commerce, the army believed that only by striking before Russia had modernised her industries and armies could Germany be preserved as the leading power in continental Europe. But Maria's mother, now with several domestic servants to assist her after her remarriage, protected the girls from these facts of political life. She gave herself over to maintaining a respectable household where the emphasis was above all on maintaining the place in society that her stepfather's rank demanded. Displays of emotion, any emotion, were forbidden, the word of the man of the house was law, the servants were scolded for any lapse from perfection in the running of the house, and Wilhelmine was nothing if not a demanding mistress of the house. She would restain the parquet flooring if the servants had failed to bring it to gleaming perfection, and would tolerate no failings from them in any part of their duties. Not surprisingly, they kept their distance from the two girls and Maria had no strong recollections of any of them.

The re-won status Wilhelmine's new marriage gave her was rudely snatched away again when outside forces beyond control of the family swept away all that they held dear.

The moment of war's arrival was etched deep on Maria's mind by one telling loss, that of the first person to whom she had been able to express her innermost feelings and thoughts, her French teacher at school. After two delicious years when she had showered this young teacher with gifts and rapt adoration, she suddenly disappeared from Maria's life forever. As the pupils assembled at school in the late summer of 1914, her eyes looked up and down the rows of teachers seated above on the stage at assembly. She fainted when she saw that Marguerite Breguand was not there and the awful truth dawned: she was French and they were now at war with France, she had become the enemy. From the very first, the war changed the atmosphere at school completely. The girls were put to work knitting jumpers and mittens for the troops in field grey, school hours were extended so that they spent at least two hours on these tasks. By the following summer, when they returned to school after another glorious sun-filled break, the girls were urged to include in their prayers the imprecation, 'May God punish England'. But Maria's lips stayed hermetically sealed. She clung to the delicacies of the French language when it was suddenly forbidden to speak this reminder of the foe's culture. European nations like England

and Italy were still held in the highest esteem by the independently minded schoolgirl even though they all willed the German soldiers to be victorious and the war to end.

Maria had certainties to hold onto, with her father's early death she could cling to his way of life and moral code, the code of the professional officer who showed no petty malice, who appreciated the strengths of his enemy at the same time as he carried out his duty. The summer of 1915 presented an opportunity to put his commands into action in a way that marked her out from her classmates forever afterwards.

The whole school had gone to a summer camp. Nearby was a prisoner-of-war camp where many French prisoners were held. They went to look at the captives in the curious way of young 13-year old girls, bold and at the same time shy. Maria saw the misery and despair stamped on their unmoving forms as she reflected on the glories of a summer day that was also the French national holiday, Bastille Day. The triumphs of French culture, explained to her patiently in the many long conversations she had had with Marguerite for a period of more than two years, became unbearably vivid. She realised what dreadful punishment it was to lose one's freedom, especially for these men who were the flower of young French manhood. She was gripped by a power stronger than herself. After her schoolmates had left, chattering gaily and collecting wild flowers, she contrived to stay behind, still quietly regarding the men shut up like animals behind the barbed wire of the camp. She gathered great handfuls of wild white flowers and approached the line of the fence, sure that no one was around to see her. She found herself standing right up to the wire looking through at the men, who did not appear to even see her, so unmoving were they.

She stretched a hand through and held out some flowers, saying in her best French,

'Aujourdhui, c'est le jour de Bastille, prenez les fleurs, s'il vous plait.'

No one spoke or moved. She despaired, but kept holding the flowers through the wire. Then a hand snatched the flowers, she held out more. These, too, were taken by the sullen men, they cried and she cried as she handed through all the flowers and then left running to rejoin her classmates. She thought no one had seen her, but the next day discovered this to be not so. She was reported by one of the parents and from then on no one in the school was allowed to speak to her as punishment for talking to the enemy.

Wilhelmine von Losch was determined to protect her two girls as best as she could from a world that had turned grey and forbidding. After the early atmosphere of carnival and festivity - the crowds had cheered the young soldiers leaving for the battle fronts convinced that right was on their side and that they would soon prevail against the plot of France and Russia to take away Germany's wealth and prestige - the dread impact of men killing each other like machines reached through to the civilians. Many of the waiting wives, including Wilhelmine, would visit the town hall to examine the posted notices detailing who was missing in action. She checked that her husband, who had been posted to the Russian front, was not among them. Dressed in black, while the girls wore grey, they solemnly filed into the corridor where the long lists of names were typewritten and hung for perusal by the patient women, who with infinite courtesy passed each other as if in a dream, each wrapped in their thoughts, each fearing the worst and hoping for the best. Many times the von Losch family visited the town hall and emerged with that strange joy that comes from not being one of those families whose nearest and dearest have been taken from them. Early on they lost an uncle, but Colonel von Losch was never on the lists of wounded, missing or dead. By 1917, the war had lost all meaning, so many families, indeed almost every family, had lost a member. Blinds were drawn in houses in every street as a mark of mourning. The family's diet, which from the beginning of the war had largely consisted of vegetables, mostly potatoes, was reduced still further. Turnips were the main food staple, with precious little else to augment the meagre rations. Grandmother Felsing often visited the house and was unfailingly cheerful in front of the two girls, and the cousins who often came round to help. She was a breath of the old Berlin, she rode each morning and always dressed in the most feminine of fashions. She wore the most beguiling perfumes and was the essence of the German society lady, as became the daughter of a respected family jewellers. She never let her standards slip and held such sway over her daughter Wilhelmine that it was like royalty visiting when she called at the exact hour she had arranged. Maria's face was becoming paler and more listless as the months of meagre rations persisted and worsened inexorably while victory stayed ever more distant. But before the grandmother's visits Wilhelmine pinched Maria and Elisabeth's cheeks to inject some colour into them. Maria was sure she noticed the wanness of her looks, but in Grandma Felsing's world no emotions were ever betrayed and the performance expected of one's station in the world was all.

The full horror of the war came home that year of 1917 when Maria's cousin Hans came to visit the family from the front. He said to Wilhelmine that Maria was growing up, and the mother immediately realised that it was a reference to her younger daughter's budding womanhood. But it was a womanhood expressed by the loving care with which she washed and laundered his field grey shirts, shirts that soon, once more, would be covered in mud and, quite possibly, blood. His announcement of her womanhood was also his farewell Maria sensed, it was his last leave before violent death struck. And so it was to be. There were heroes in the family too. Another uncle led the first Zeppelin raid on London, but Maria now felt she did not care how the war ended, as long as it ended. When her mother whispered that the Americans were joining the war and that all was lost for Germany, Maria knew she was right and was secretly glad it was all going to come to an end. The coming defeat was made all the more bitter for Wilhelmine, because she had only just learnt her second husband had been wounded on the Russian front. She travelled to see him, and he seemed likely to recover before a secondary infection struck him down, as it struck down many of those wounded but not killed on the battlegrounds.

Maria's life was given over to getting through each day, school lessons continued as though everything was normal, but by the time of the war's end when she was about to turn 16, she already knew that the old way of life would not return. She had seen the deformed and crippled men flooding back on the hospital trains that brought the still mud and blood covered troops into the heart of Berlin. She could see with her own eyes the blind and gassed men begging on Berlin's streets. She shared the tears of widows and orphans, her friends and neighbours. Berlin was seething with a strange kind of anger as the streets filled with the returning soldiers on the declaration of the Armistice. Maria went out with her sister to see this great mass of young men, for four years she had lived almost exclusively in female company. It was a bitter shock to see them. Where there had been the bloom of youth and mischievousness, now there was a greyness on their faces, they were like ghosts staring into the distance who could not be touched.

The bitterness and frustration of the troops upon their return to the capital soon turned to violence, it was the only life they now knew. Street gangs began fighting one another, new political parties were formed to run the country as the Kaiser fled to exile in Holland and the full impact of the Armistice became clearer. At first, the people were told there had been an honourable truce to stop the fighting, later it became clear Germany had been defeated. The shops had even less food in them, so much less that on every street corner there were crowds of beggars beseeching the passers-by for scraps. But Maria had none to give. Thanks to her mother's family, and the wealth put aside from the good days in the jewellery business, Wilhelmine managed to provide for the girls, but it was a close run thing. Over half a million starved to death in Germany, and as many more died from the influenza that was sweeping the country in the wake of the defeat. It was as though the military disaster and the despair it brought was also enacted in each individual, they gave up on life and it ebbed away from them. To Maria it became clearer that only an iron discipline passed on by her father could protect against this external chaos.

Her mother decided that she must leave Berlin, which was becoming ever more dangerous, with people killed in riots and brawls every day, it was so commonplace that it rated no more than a couple of lines in the daily newspapers which now announced that a revolutionary committee had taken over, only for the leader to be killed by his rivals within a few months. The army fought to bring back some discipline into national life, for the crowds had descended into a rabble. The 16-year-old started to hope they would be successful in restoring the old order.

Wilhelmine removed her younger daughter to a boarding school in the old city of Weimar where both Goethe and Schiller had lived. It was a centre of German high culture in a world that had, apparently, gone mad. Here there were no street demonstrations and battles, Maria could study violin and German culture under expert tutors in the company of other young ladies whose parents were determined that they would be equipped with all the traditional German graces for when normality returned.

Maria immersed herself in her studies of the great poets, learning many of Goethe's poems by heart, while his description of troubled youth left her sure that she was not as alone as she imagined. The strength of Goethe's thinking and his ideals gave her an idol to emulate, especially now that she had no father or stepfather to learn from. She wandered the streets he had wandered, enjoyed her first flush of freedom and became increasingly proficient with her violin playing. Her English violin tutor at home in Berlin had been the first to tell her mother she had gifts for playing this most demanding of musical instruments. To assist her in Weimar was a handsome, still quite young, music teacher, Professor Reitz, who she made her special friend by running his errands for him, and bringing him small gifts.

While in Weimar, Maria made a visit to the town of Garmisch, where she had learnt her film heroine, Henny Porten, had a beautiful house. Seized by a boldness or an infatuation that took her over completely, Maria stood under the actress's window and played her favourite music. Henny Porten did not come to the window to acknowledge her fan, instead she shut it. But Maria had a strange presentiment in the empty street. One day she would have as devoted a following as Henny had, but she would also honour and reward her fans loyalty.

It was the male attractions of her music professor which induced Maria to leave behind the innocence of girlhood. One day he allowed her to kiss him when she presented him with some fruit as one of her little gifts. The kiss was prolonged, he took her in his arms and initiated her into the ways of love there and then on his sofa. The bristle hair of the sofa ground against her soft skin as the professor forcibly took her in spite of her spirited resistance. It was an uncomfortable experience, she decided she did not enjoy being penetrated. After that pupil and teacher met secretly every week, until one day her mother visited Weimar unexpectedly. Maria was floating around on air, in love, drinking in the magic of the great poets and musicians who had lived in the enchanted town. After the grey of the war years, each day was drenched in colour and promise and the inspired essences of the richness of life. Her secret rapture showed all too clearly to her mother who insisted she leave immediately, keenly aware that scandal threatened, that her secret would soon be out and the only way to protect her reputation was to withdraw her and have no further contact with the school or her schoolfriends. Wilhelmine took back from Weimar a young woman who had tasted the world, and the taste was good.

Chapter Two

The Berlin Cabaret

Maria Magdalena returned to Berlin just in time for her 19th birthday, but the changes in the city since she had been away were extraordinary. It was only two years since the war had come to an end, but in that time the Berliners had become 'devil may care'. There were thousands of Russians, Poles, Slovakians, Austrians, Danes, Italians and many more nationalities to be found on every street corner, in every pavement café. Where before there had been a Prussian sense of decorum and order, now the air was filled with a cacophony of different languages, accents and philosophies. The Russians were a very distinguished cast of aristocratic refugees, all the more poignant for their sudden fall from grace. But, in truth, the catastrophe had happened for Maria's world of civilised values as well. Starvation stalked the streets of Berlin for those unfortunate enough to have no resources to fall back on, and she counted herself lucky that Wilhelmine had her brother Hasso, who ran the Felsing jewellery shop, to call upon if their meagre rations proved insufficient to keep body and soul together.

She wandered the streets for her first few months back in a daze, hardly able to take in the enormous changes she saw all about, torn by a desire to help the poor who heartbreakingly lined fashionable streets like Kurfurstendamm and all the other main thoroughfares leading off from the Brandenburg Gate. But slowly she got caught up in the mad excitement of these strange crowds of émigrés mingled with the many German poor. She noted grimly the pitiless treatment that befell the war wounded. Men with no legs, no arms, no eyes, haunted the streets selling matchboxes, offering shoe shines, plaintively playing their music from accordions and violins. She felt enormously privileged when her mother bought her a violin for 2,500 marks - a fabulous sum in those days, it would have bought a cheap house in the Berlin suburbs. It was her mother's compensation for taking her away from her professorial lover and Weimar where she had come to appreciate the great achievements of its poets and musicians. But all was not well between Wilhelmine and Maria.

In Maria's early days her mother had a pet name for her, 'Pauli', because she had wanted a boy to follow on from her elder sister, Elisabeth, who was training to be a teacher. Wilhelmine was determined that the career she had plumped her heart on for her younger daughter, as a violinist, should allow no distractions and Maria was enrolled in Berlin's top high school for music where she was made to practise Bach hour after hour. As often happens to girls growing out of their teens she began to wonder where this training was going to lead, where her happiness was to be found. She started to row with her mother, neglect the practice of music for the reading of Germany's great poets, especially Rilke who entranced her with the magic of his words. She dreamt of being able to spellbind people with speech as he did with his writing. She wondered what her long dead father would have advised her to do when these moods of black despair came upon her and she could see no end to the sterile playing of the violin at a school she had begun to hate. After the magic of Weimar, the traditional Prussian school with its emphasis on endless repetition and technique seemed designed to kill all the youthful joie de vivre she wished to express. She mourned the sudden parting from her revered music teacher and nothing her mother could say convinced Maria that Wilhelmine had acted in her best interests. The dark clouds in her mind grew ever larger, she wandered the streets in an agony of despair as she saw the world she believed in visibly crumbling. There were no fine carriages on the streets gently perambulating along as in her girlhood. In their place, huge automobiles plied up and down the wide thoroughfares, with their owners displaying the sudden wealth they had acquired in the cacophony that was business in the city. She knew, even in her innocence, that many of these people were war profiteers who had grown fat on the troops' misery. They showed no thought at all for the wretches begging in the gutters and doorways, but ostentatiously swept past with only concern for themselves. She envied their magnificent display at the same time as she could see the evident corruption black money brought into their hearts. Money itself was rapidly losing any value. The price of any scraps of food, when they could be found on the market stalls, multiplied week by week till a week's wages bought merely a few potatoes and greens, the only certainty being that by the next week the prices would have doubled again. Her mother tried to shield her from the grim reality, but she began to change into a cynical worldly wise 19-year-old who accepted the new dispensation with its new laws of survival, she was just a face in the crowd that pushed and jostled, forsook all manners and grabbed for what it could.

After the long hours of violin practice Maria took to visiting the pavement cafés all along Kurfurstendamm in the afternoons and wondering at the foibles of the passing parade of humanity. There was a new mood of desperate gaiety which café society adopted to laugh off the chaos they could sense all around. There was new money where once there had been old certainties. Those who had cash were tough businessmen, totally ruthless in obtaining what they wanted. She began to experiment with her clothes. Long feather boas were the last word in fashion, a statement that you were part of sophisticated café society, unshocked by any of the sights you saw on the Berlin streets. There were people murdered in front of the crowds, usually in angry fights where jeering people surrounded the combatants. The police appeared to be powerless to stop the descent into mayhem.

Defeat weighed hard upon the proud Berliners, no one believed in anything, except getting through the day and losing oneself in drink or drugs or quick flirtations. Maria noted how girls her own age flaunted themselves in shorter and shorter skirts, wide open blouses, facing strangers with a leer on their lips and a sparkle in their eye. Suddenly, you could speak to whoever you wanted, no introductions were necessary and she quickly caught on to the new code. One day in the spring she was walking past the Café Nationale where girls of easy repute were well known to be available. Some even sat at the tables with bare breasts as they shamelessly exposed their assets. But with the low wages now virtually worthless, the people had to fall back on other more personal assets. She passed a pale faced young man in the crowd and smiled, he stopped and soon they were in ecstatic communication. She found herself suggesting they go to his flat nearby and pass the afternoon in each other's company. There was an aura about his pale skin and clear eyes she found irresistibly attractive. He became the first lover of her own age, and she found he welcomed her taking the lead in their mutual discovery of the joys of the flesh. Little did she realise that the pallor of his skin which so attracted her and matched her own fair skin was a sign of a fatal disease that was wasting him away. Before her eyes over the few weeks of spring they were together he gradually weakened until one day she found him dead from what the doctors diagnosed as dysentery. Death was very much present in this new Berlin, if not from influenza or starvation, then the gangs promised and delivered a violent end to life as they each sought to control the streets as a prelude to political power.

By the summertime, the small amount of money Maria's mother gave her each week was no longer enough to even purchase coffee and apple cake in the fashionable cafés. She was forced to search out any type of work to help buy the fabulous new fashions she saw being flaunted all around her by young women who always appeared to have a rich businessman to accompany them. She found work in a glove factory, then needed more money still so that in the evenings she also worked in a hat shop, when even this was not enough to produce a living wage she worked in a news kiosk early in the mornings as well. The hustle and bustle of the streets became her life from morning till night. It was strangely thrilling for a girl who had had such a sheltered upbringing. But it was also exhausting.

Maria noticed they always seemed to need musicians in the cabaret clubs that were opening up all over Berlin, as well as the picture palaces that were even more popular. Motion pictures were soon as fashionable an entertainment as the animated conversations of café society. But Berlin's cabaret clubs held the greatest attraction for her, they were very risqué places, certainly not the kind that her mother would ever have dreamt she would dare frequent. But an increasing boldness was upon her as she realised it was up to her whether she sank or swam in the increasing madness all around. She played in the pits in an orchestra accompanying the films. Her legs caught the eye of the conductor who introduced her to a club where topless dancers came on as a break between the political satire and the popular songs. It was really a continuation of the old music halls, but now people liked their entertainment to be more intimate in some darkened cellar. She was taken on to play violin in several of the clubs and found a way to mix in the kind of circles previously forbidden to someone of her class and background. But a part of her sought the limelight rather than the dark pits where the musicians were placed. She had not too long a time to wait before she found herself providing the entertainment rather than accompanying it.

Maria had another brief taste of love in the cabaret club. A devastatingly handsome businessman, some 15 years older than herself who was possessed of the wit and sophistication that Berliners have always valued in their companions. It was her naivete that led her to presume she had no competitors for his affections. After a whirlwind romance in which he bedded her and taught her, even encouraging her to sit astride him in cafés so that they could take their pleasure wherever it pleased them, she discovered she was not his only girlfriend. He confessed - though he saw little wrong with it - that he had a wife, and several other girlfriends as well.

'We are friends, that is all, what more do you want?' he asked her.

She told him she could not share him with other young girls, his staying with his wife she could understand, but if a man was to have her, he must be devoted to her, under her spell, that was always her aim, even if I she were far away in place and time. She wanted to hold a special place in his heart, leave her inner essence as an image in his brain.

Almost on the rebound from this second romance, she met a girl who she could admire and learn from. A young girl like herself discovering the new post-war Berlin. Her name was Gerda Huba, an aspiring writer who had a job as a librarian. She immediately proposed that Maria move in with her and share the tiny two rooms she occupied in the poor Wilmersdorf part of town. Maria's mother took the news in a resigned fashion, she knew her younger daughter was spending more and more time in the cafés, less and less at home with her music, but realised she was approaching 20 and no longer the sweet innocent of even a year before.

It was Gerda who opened Maria's eyes to the realities of the new post-war Berlin. She was better read than Maria, despised women who allowed themselves to be dictated to by men and argued that the war and its aftermath had changed everything. Their responsibility was to themselves, there was no higher power ordaining their roles, the ruling class (and she included Maria's parents in this category) had lost their power and sway over the people. They and their strict codes of behaviour were consigned to the dustbin of history. Gerda was an idealistic socialist excited by the great movements of liberation springing up all over Europe. There was talk of revolution on the streets of Berlin, and Paris, London, Glasgow, Munich, Milan... the whole continent was in ferment in 1921, most obviously in Russia where a bitter battle raged between the Red and White armies after the assassination of the Czar and his family. Germany's own Kaiser lived in ignominy in Holland and the old imperial aristocratic families were being reduced by the ever spiralling inflation into genteel poverty.

Gerda attracted Maria with the dangerous thoughts she dared to utter. In Maria she claimed to see an example of the fallen ruling class. Maria laughed at this conceit, reflecting on the privations of the war years. The two young women shared the meagre rooms, and the even more meagre meals. They were inseparable as they gathered confirmation all around them of the rightness of their new revolutionary philosophy.

They walked along the crowded streets and thoroughfares arm in arm, Maria head over heels in love with Gerda's mind, besotted with her view of the world, her all devouring logic, her marvellous encyclopaedic knowledge which contrasted so much with her very sheltered background. On the street corners they laughed and giggled at the women openly soliciting business dressed in outrageous ringmaster uniforms, shiny black boots, fishnet stockinged legs, riding whips nonchalantly held in the cleft of their arms. The burlesque women sought men who would pay handsomely to be humiliated and did a roaring trade among the ever more blatant passers-by who, with no work to distract them, sought temporary relief in novelty while they still had some money to their name. The women affected a masculine commanding appearance, especially the many apparently respectable housewives who travelled into the town from the suburbs to desperately try and eke out their housekeeping money. The two young women spent much of their free time in the cafeterias and clubs, where homosexuals openly displayed their affections as they sat, chattered, laughed and observed the foibles of humanity through the day. There were men fawning at prospective clients over fluttering fans, their eyes darkly made up even in the middle of the day. The two friends went to clubs where naked girls danced with their patrons in mocking tea dances - all pretence that the assignations were for anything other than quick relief from the doomed economy outside the doors was dropped.

Maria fell under this fatalistic spell. If she saw a man across the table who she liked, a quick wink, a girlish giggle, and an invitation to go to his flat (or hers) ended the pleasantries of the afternoon in a frenzied burst of lovemaking. Clothes and inhibitions were shed daily and nightly all over Berlin, the pace of the Jazz Age had begun to assert itself and Berlin was where it found its first expression. The city claimed with some justification to be 'the fastest in the world.' Some of the cabaret clubs openly allowed their guests to try drugs like cocaine and marijuana, opium and heroin, although Maria avoided these indulgences. She looked into the eyes of the drugged people and saw they were trying to blot out the reality all around them, whereas she found it all strangely exciting and alluring, with the hint of danger added to the mix. A dark current had entered Berliners' lives, and it fed them an energy and an appetite for further thrills. The cabarets lasted long into the night, Gerda and she would return at dawn to their rooms ready, after a few hours sleep, to throw ourselves into the social whirl once more. Maria hardly saw her mother, who presumed she was regularly attending music school, although her daughter had become a very infrequent visitor to the lessons which were so removed from the reality of life in café society.

The need for money and independence led Maria to take her courage in both hands one day at a club where she played in the orchestra. She suggested to the owner she join the chorus girls he had just begun auditioning. He asked her to show him her legs which she quite brazenly did, hoisting her skirts up above the waist so that he was dazzled by her underwear. He asked her to give a few high kicks which again flashed the frilly underwear before his wondering eyes. That was enough, she was in, a member of the man's 'Thielscher Girls', twelve in number. Over the autumn and winter of 1921 to 1922 they visited Hamburg and Cologne as well as clubs around Berlin. There were other things beside violin playing, she realised, that could help a young woman progress in the world of entertainment. The chorus line proved her most regular source of income.

The excursion into the cabaret was all that a girl who had just turned 20 could wish for. She already knew the theatre was what she was intended for, not the concert hall. On the stage she came alive, revelled in the attention the kicking chorus line generated with flowers raining upon them as they roused the audience to cheers of delight at their increasingly daring routines. They wore top hats and tight body hugging costumes, decked out in feathers around their waists, with white silk stockings completing the revealing outfits. The girls in the troupe were all like her, surviving from day to day. They were often invited to parties where drink flowed and food was all about. After the rigours of the day when buying the next meal could cost a week's earnings it was an enchanted world. Those who still had money were quite happy to finance the parties as long as everyone had a good time. It was usually dawn by the time she made her way back to the two shabby rooms, often with several of the girls in the chorus line joining her since they had nowhere to go.

A few hours sleep, and the other woman reappeared, the dutiful violin student attending her lessons at the High School, but Maria had joined other lessons for voice production which were also held at the school. She longed to be able to captivate an audience with her voice rather than her music, and just as in the cabaret she came to realise that it is, above all, the personality of a performer which attracts and fascinates. She was determined to find an outlet for the commanding theatrical face she wanted to show the world.

Eventually she told her anxious mother that her wrist muscles were permanently damaged by the constant violin practice, that it was no use pretending she could follow this as a career, and so she had decided to become an actress. Wilhelmine took the news badly. Since Maria's return to Berlin she had feared the changes in her daughter and disapproved of her new friends and lifestyle profoundly. Wilhelmine had hoped Maria would soon grow out of her madcap stage. But the mother's concerns were ignored until she became resigned to Maria's desire to go on the stage, even as she pointed out it was no profession for a young woman of Maria's breeding and background. For mama, the war had changed nothing, she clung to her Prussian ways. But one day she surprised Maria by saying that Uncle Willi, from the family jewellery shop, had offered to help get her a film test.

Maria was ecstatic. The motion picture business was booming all over Berlin, there were many more picture palaces than there were clubs or theatres, but in the snobbery of the Berlin arts world the motion pictures were not considered a serious art form, just a cheap escapist entertainment for the downtrodden masses. However, the great attraction of the new film studios was their ability to pay wages far in excess of anything that could be expected in the theatre. Maria arrived one day in April at the studios to await her film test.

The gate people told her she would have to wait until the day's filming was complete before she could meet Stefan Lorant. Eventually, he came out of the hothouse of the film studio where, because they worked under glass, the atmosphere created by the heat of the lamps was like a tropical greenhouse. He was exhausted by the day's shooting.

'Is it possible you could come back another day?' he asked in a weary way when she introduced herself, bubbling over with enthusiasm and quite prepared to give the performance of her life.

'I feel I am meant to work in films, it is my only wish in life,' she melodramatically told him.

'The heat inside the studio is too much, we have been there all day, it is brutal work, not at all the glamourous life you would imagine,' he replied.

'Why not do your test out here?' she countered, fixing him with a relentless look of seriousness, 'I will not disappoint you. My mother Wilhelmina von Losch said that you would not let down the sister of Willy Felsing.'

This appeal to his duty persuaded the young film director.

'Very well, we will do the test out here,' he conceded.

He sent for a camera and tripod while he scanned about him with an eagle eye.

'You see that fence there?' he said, indicating the edge of the film production company's lot, 'I want you to jump off there and smile at the same time.'

Maria did as she was bid.

'Now grimace. Now shout and fling out your arms.'

A crowd of actors and actresses gathered as he put her through her paces. They enjoyed watching the director manipulate her like a marionette in his hand, as she jumped and returned, jumped and returned more than a dozen times. Finally, he called a halt.

'We will get in touch if we wish to pursue your interest, Fraulein von Losch,' he said.

Turning to his friends gathered around, who had hugely enjoyed the spectacle of the young eager girl obeying his whim like a pet dog she heard him say.

'There's no need to look at the test, I can tell you now, there's nothing there. But those wide cheek bones, those expressionless eyes, that is a haunted look, strange for one so young.'

Maria heard nothing more, but the rejection made her all the more determined.

Her work with the Thielscher Girls resulted in offers of modelling for advertisements. Always, her legs had to be displayed while she coquettishly held the manufacturer's wares. There is a photo which still exists of a record she promoted, it is held delicately above her belly, her garter showing on long shapely legs, her gloved hands holding the record in tender adoration while she coyly gazes at the camera. The chemise-like short dress leaves little to be imagined, it is daring even by today's standards. In early 1920s Berlin, it was the last word in sophistication. And sophistication was what every young Berlin girl aspired to portray. A worldly wise knowingness, not shy young blooms but women of the world. Underneath the surface they were just having a good time and found it all highly amusing. Women were allowed to display their attractions and revelled at the opportunity after so many years of grinding dullness and disaster.

Chapter Three

Love and Marriage

It took Maria Magdalene some time to get over her disappointment with the film test, but slowly the realisation dawned that she needed training if she were to be an actress. She felt a natural affinity with the stage, even at school she had been allowed to play a few parts and had cultivated a gypsy style of dressing with her hair allowed to flow in profusion in contrast to the more Prussian severity most of her school contemporaries favoured. The time could not have been more appropriate. Film production companies were arising all over Berlin as the fledgling motion pictures of pre-War days became a mass medium and early reservations about their suitability for respectable people crumbled before the lure of seeing dreams played out on a screen, even if there were problems with the flickering picture registering anything more than an approximation to reality. However, these new companies were not prepared to take a chance on untrained amateurs. Professionalism was as important as looks. There were any number of girls who dreamed of becoming movie stars - the talk was of hardly anything else in the cafés. Who was acting in what film? Who was recruiting extras? Who was destined for stardom? These were the burning questions. The young would-be actress decided to mould herself into a motion picture star and began by changing her name. From 1922 onwards, she was always Marlene Dietrich, as she reverted back to her real father's name and dropped von Losch forever. Even as a child she had already decided her stage name would be Marlene, rather than Maria Magdalene, and this became her permanent Christian name. It unlocked the real personality who had languished in the shadows in the war years and afterwards. With her father's name reclaimed, she reverted to his determined organised way of conducting oneself, and gradually left behind the period of drifting that she had entered on her return to Berlin. The period of questioning and doubt was over and a splendid butterfly was to emerge from the unpromising chrysalis.

Marlene had learned on the café society grapevine that the best school for actresses was run by an Austrian Jew, Max Reinhardt (he had changed his name from Goldmann to sound more German). He used the actors and actresses he had trained to perform in his own theatres, and the numerous film companies circulated the school with details of their requirements for extras and small bit parts in their films. To gain entrance to the school it was necessary to perform some theatrical pieces and one day in late spring of 1922 she arrived - inwardly quaking - at the school which was situated on the top floor of one of Max Reinhardt's four Berlin theatres. There were dozens of girls milling about, all eager to be taken on at the prestigious academy and she immediately realised she would have to attract the attention of the teachers in some way. There were a dozen girls lined up away from the makeshift stage. They had been told to recite a piece from a play or poem of their choice, and then to perform Gretchen's prayer from Goethe's Faust. Marlene was convinced her heavenly muse, Goethe, would guide her in her performance after the long days of adoration in Weimar.

The first piece was very close to her heart, she saw herself as the spirit of a dead girl speaking to a dying nobleman who in her imagination easily became her dying father - it was from Hugo von Hofmannsthal's mystical piece, *Der Tor und der Tod - 'Death and the Fool'*.

'Your letter came, the last, the dreadful one; And then I wished to die.
One letter more I meant to write in parting; No lament, not passionate or fierce unbridled grief But just to make you yearn a little for me.'

This recitation was received with polite murmurings among the assembled teachers.

'Thank you. Now recite Gretchen's prayer,' called a voice out of the gloom.

'On your knees please.'

She stood fixed to the spot, unprepared for this command to kneel.
A pillow sailed through the air and landed at her feet.

'What is this for?' she asked coquettishly, playing the innocent dumb girl.

'So you can kneel,' said the teacher patiently.

She knelt, taking care to maintain her dignity, and recited poor Gretchen's prayer, it was as if she were her, seeking release from the uncertainties of her life.

After the dozen girls were auditioned, some were told they had been accepted. No one came to tell Marlene she could join the school but the teacher who had thrown the cushion at her feet came over. He was relaxed and very confident, she immediately felt weak at the knees in his presence, he was the key to her future she realised.

'You look like an actress,' he began, 'but you have no natural talent for it that I can see, you will have to work at it.'

She smiled, willing to admit she needed teaching.

'Can you teach me then?' she asked.

'The school only has very limited vacancies. But I do hold private classes for individual girls, perhaps that would help you to be accepted by the school.'

She understood the drift of the conversation, it had echoes of her music teacher in Weimar's approach to bestowing his knowledge for a price. Private lessons began the next day and included a brief passionate encounter in a small room at the back of the theatre. The teacher, Berthold Held, was a friend and colleague of Reinhardt, he explained, after their brief but ecstatic coupling against a wall where he unceremoniously hoisted her skirts and entered her with little preliminary delicacies. He took it as a matter of course that a grateful young actress would show her affection in a physical way and she took care not to disappoint him. It was just like the times with her music teacher, she played the helpless pupil while the older man initiated her into the ways of love, or so he thought. By now, she was rapidly gaining experience in this theatre of life and knew how to satisfy a man by gushing all over him, they almost always welcomed her taking the lead after the initial seduction where she was meek and passive. She made sure Berthold would remember her as she frantically worked herself against him.

After a month, the flames of the affair were cooling. Berthold and Marlene were good friends. He made sure she joined the regular acting classes and was accepted as a full member of the school. Another girl joined the classes at the same time as her, Grete Mosheim. Marlene discovered that they had shared Berthold's favours, that he had told Grete exactly the same as her, that she had the looks of an actress but no talent. Berthold took great delight in introducing the two girls. 'You have a lot in common,' he enigmatically stated with a half smile. In no time at all they were great friends, and confided their secrets to each other.

Although Max Reinhardt's School of Drama was essentially a training ground for his four theatres, all the young actors and actresses were well aware of the growing attraction of the motion pictures. Marlene did not pretend to understand the economics of the situation, for her own finances were so bad she had to return home, not even able to finance her share of the rooms in Kaiserallee with Gerda Huba. Her mother suffered in silence as Marlene told her of her plans to be an actress. Wilhelmine was certain it was the beginning of a downward path, in her mind only women of easy virtue became stage - or worse - screen actresses.

One day, for a dare, Marlene managed to get an introduction for Grete Mosheim and herself to meet Georg Jacoby, who they heard was casting for parts in an historical romance comedy *Der kleine Napoleon - 'Little Napoleon'*. Well aware of how young actresses could get the attention of a director, Marlene laughed and joked with him, displaying all her newly acquired Berlin wit and self-confidence. He appreciated the good humour, for to her astonishment he agreed that both Grete and she could have small parts in the film, her very first. He was not exaggerating about the smallness either. She appeared in just one scene as a lady's maid which required her to be on set for just a few days in August. But those few days of bright sunlight and good humoured camaraderie she discovered at the studios made her more determined than ever to make motion pictures her career. It was confirmed for her when she met Stefan Lorant in the street, he asked how her film career was progressing. Less gauche than the previous year, and also a little less innocent, she simply told him that her progress was slow but that she would persevere.

Then a rare invitation arrived at the drama school - the girls were invited to come to a casting session for a major new film production by Joe May. The invitation was signed by Rudolf Sieber, his young assistant. Marlene made a note of the name and went to the casting session with Grete Mosheim. To catch the eye of the casting director, who she was surprised to find was only about 25 but tall blond and handsome, she fluttered her eyes, flailed a feather boa about her neck, carried a small dog in her arms and turned her easy flowing charm in his direction. There were a dozen girls who had gone from the school and as usual the session ended with a 'We'll let you know.' But Rudolf Sieber motioned to Marlene to follow him into a room where the director himself, Joe May, was shown the new discovery by the casting director. He told her to turn, smile, act like a street courtesan and be provocative. All this came naturally to an habitué of the Kurfurstendamm cafés and she knew he was impressed, though by now Marlene had learnt to hide her enthusiasm under a guise of having done this many times before. Rudolf Sieber was keen to have some of the crowd scenes played by 'amateurs' rather than trained actors and actresses to make it more authentic, so he was not worried by her lack of movie experience, although she made much of having just finished work on *'Little Napoleon'.* Unlike that film, *Tragodie der Liebe - 'Tragedy of Love'* - was a big production with one of Germany's leading actors, Emil Jannings, in the starring role. The story revolved around Jannings standing trial as a wrestler who was led into committing murder. The film captures the mood of the times, as it portrays criminals in gambling casinos where violence permeates their every move. Since inflation was roaring ahead ever faster and a meal now cost a million marks, that was indeed the situation on the streets. It was everyone for himself, the only way to survive, and many were not, the destitute grew ever larger in number in Berlin, amidst the cacophony of expensive cars forcing their way through thoroughfares where people were selling their last few precious possessions in competition with each other. Street hawkers attempted to sell every imaginable knickknack to the thousands of refugees and unemployed aimlessly walking up and down. It was a kind of bedlam. But once you got used to the constant commotion it had a raw edge of dangerous excitement, a sense of vitality had returned to the streets after the sense of futility which had been all pervading just two years before.

The day after the audition, while at home, Marlene was stunned to hear Rudolf Sieber talking to her mother at the door. Wilhelmine ushered him in.

When the film shooting was too soon over, Rudolf began calling to take her to the film parties to which he was regularly invited since he was regarded as someone with much influence. Her mother remained stiff and reserved with him, even insisting that she return home at a reasonable hour. In spite of the deteriorating economic situation, somehow the people on the fringe of the film world still had the money for lavish parties where wine and food were in abundance, and many experimented with drugs like cocaine and opium as well. Marlene went against her mother's wishes and accompanied

Rudolf everywhere. He found the restrictions her mother tried to place on them vexing in the extreme.

'I could have any girl I want,' he said one night, 'there are thousands of beautiful Russian girls trying to get into films, and your mother wants me to act like an old fashioned Prussian!'

Marlene was terrified that Rudolf would quickly become bored with her and return to his former womanising ways but he seemed content to take her to the theatres where she had small supporting parts to play after drama lessons all day. These parts were unpaid, it was expected that the school's pupils would gain practical experience as part of their drama course. When Rudolf was busy on his film work as an assistant Marlene made her own way all over Berlin by bus and subway, sometimes appearing in three bit parts in three different plays in one night. She was overflowing with an energy that allowed her to do all this and stay up half the night at a post-play party before reappearing dutifully at the Drama School the next morning.

By the winter, everyone in Berlin was feeling the impact of the inflationary spiral. You ate when you could, those who somehow held on to their possessions were suspected of being involved in shady deals, but no one any longer asked questions or tried to preserve a front of respectability, the casualties were too numerous and too near to home for that. One night she took some coal and some scraps of food from her mother's pantry and made her way over to Rudolf's flat. When he trudged in after a hard day, he found a warm fire and a meal to welcome him, with Marlene as the delicious dessert. In that tough winter of early 1923 it was enough to seem like heaven, from this time on she had won over the heart of Rudolf, his other glamorous women did not provide for his creature comforts like her. It was the very practical hausfrau approach to men.

By the spring they were married. The couple had a civil wedding in the town hall of Berlin-Friednau on the 17 May,

1923, with many of Marlene's relatives present but fewer of Rudolf's. She was 21, he was 26. Her hopes, like those of every young girl at that age, were to have a loving relationship blessed with a family, although she always presumed this could be combined with a career in motion pictures.

The month before the wedding she had her third film part when, recommended by Rudolf, she had been cast as a peasant girl by Wilhelm Dieterle in his film D*er Mensch am Wege - 'Man by the Roadside'*. His only requirement was that she show plenty of leg in her peasant outfit.

'If they want legs, they can have legs,' she told him matter of factly, Berlin girls believed in being direct. Perhaps Dieterle saw her as a peasant because of the very simple lifestyle most people were forced to live. Perhaps he could detect the Swabian farm folk who had left for the attractions of Berlin a century before. The film people somehow managed to survive all the tribulations and even prosper. They did this through film sales abroad paid for in foreign currency that could purchase mountains of German paper money. Money was weighed out from suitcases and barrows as the great inflation roared away without check.

But Marlene was torn between theatre and film. The film world paid better certainly, but part of her yearned for the respectability of serious plays. Indeed, she had a small part in *'The Taming of the Shrew'* which featured the major star, Elisabeth Bergner. Marlene was so hypnotised by her performance that she nearly missed her lines each of the 42 nights that the play was performed the October before her marriage. After marriage, it was theatrical roles that came her way. She was aptly cast as a woman with the sap of life urgently rising in *Wenn der junge Wein bluht - 'When the Young Vine Blooms'*. At the rehearsals for this play she met a young actress who devastated Marlene with her powerful beauty, so much so that her young and jealous husband took to escorting her to the theatre each night and then escorting her home after the performance, so afraid was he that he would lose Marlene to her charms. But their first year of marriage was happy - even though it became clear to Marlene that Rudolf led as precarious a life as an assistant director or producer as that of any actress. She would have to rely on her own talents to make sure the household survived.

By early 1924 a meal could cost a trillion marks, the whole country appeared on the brink of collapse. Yet they carried on with their lives, fortified by the resilience and unknowingness of youth. There was only a small film part that came her way in the first part of the year, she played a two-minute part in *Der Sprung ins Leben - 'The Leap into Life'* - in July. She was a poor girl in love with a death-defying acrobat in this little melodrama, the most vivid impression it left on her was the magnificence of the ringmaster's outfit, with his shiny boots and whip, rather like the women out on the streets who increasingly resorted to the bizarre in their efforts to attract trade.

She was happy to be four months pregnant and escaped into the female world where the pulse of life can be felt and seen all around with a growing human being inside as confirmation of e melodrama, the most vivid impression it left on her was the magnificence of the ringmaster's outfit, with his shiny boots and whip, rather like the women out on the streets who increasingly resorted to the bizarre in their efforts to attract trade.

She was happy to be four months pregnant and escaped into the female world where the pulse of life can be felt and seen all around with a growing human being inside as confirmation of over from the screaming, blood- filled ordeal at home for many months. It was not until the summer of 1925 that she felt completely back to her normal zesty self and they took a carefree family holiday at Westerland on the German coast with friends. Only then did Marlene seriously contemplate her return to film work. Earlier in the year she had heard that a Swedish star was at work in Berlin at the Hirscher-Sofar Film studios and had joined one crowd scene to see the effect created by this femme fatale, a role she had tried herself in the theatre late in 1922, but Marlene was still too young to bring off the tantalising attractions of a woman with a secret (or many). Greta Garbo, yes it was she, departed for America that summer. But Marlene had seen her future during that fleeting visit to the set of 'Joyless Street'. Greta Gustaffson, renamed Garbo, had about her an air of purity and remoteness, as though a child of the heavenly stars, almost an angel, though not an innocent. What appealed to Marlene's sense of drama even more was Garbo's departure with her own Svengali figure - the mid-European Jewish film director Mauritz Stiller - immediately after the film premiere on board a ship bound first for Gothenburg and then New York. It was a splendid way to leave Europe behind for a young girl of 21 who had worked in a barbershop in Stockholm before being discovered by this middle-aged mentor who worked magic in the films he directed.

Chapter Four

First intimations of success

For nine months Marlene was content to be a mother with a growing young baby daughter and a handsome attentive father, Rudi was so delighted they had become a family that she faithfully followed the role he had allotted her of good German mother. But the lure of the film studios started to exercise its spell over her as they entered the autumn of 1925. Marlene began returning to her old haunts on the Kurfurstendamm and staying out till dawn with the film crowd, usually the more daring actresses and the hangers-on. The club scene was booming, the desperate days of runaway inflation had come to an end with currency reform. The authorities simply cut off the 12 zeros on the notes and started all over again. For some people, the great inflation had been the best of times, they had used the worthless paper to buy solid assets like houses and film studios and newspapers (this was how the majority owner of the UFA studios, Alfred Hugenburg, had prospered). It also made it very easy for the profiteers to pay off old debts when they had dwindled to insignificance in the course of a month. Banks were charging 35% interest per day on loans. Marlene, however, saw the housekeeping money dwindle to nothingness and discovered Rudi was unable to provide a regular wage even when the Americans began investing in Germany and prosperity looked as though it might be finally restored after a dozen years of despair. 'Joyless Street' had perfectly described the mood of the times, ordinary people realised that they would have to sell all they held most dear simply to survive.

The cabaret had become big business in Berlin. Marlene joined actresses like Grete Mosheim and Leni Riefenstahl in visiting the hot spots in town. It was the Leni who was to make propaganda films for Hitler. He had a desire to be seen in the company of beautiful women and Leni received a dinner invitation from Hitler in the early 1930s where he went for a walk with her in the garden of the hotel and hugged her briefly before declaring he must devote himself to saving Germany.

The women often went to the lesbian clubs. In all the clubs outrageous humour was the great attraction, even more than the wildly suggestive dances where Marlene took female partners onto the floor and made love to them in front of the unshockable audience. The bystanders cheered them on as the couple kissed and stroked, fondled and undressed each other, flaunting bodies kept in shape by visiting men's gymnasiums to go through the rigorous workouts.

Another feature of the clubs was the very heavy use of cocaine by the decadent Russians, who had background and breeding but no money at all, they buried their bitterness in temporary forgetfulness but it was never enough. Marlene saw too many people die or fall into physical disrepair to ever want to let herself go. It helped to have been brought up as a good Prussian girl from an upper class background. She could never forget her appearance, and loved to be the centre of attention walking around in short skirts to show off her legs with no brassiere or undergarments of any kind. She became practised in flinging a high kick as she danced the tango to tantalise the watching men with a brief flash of womanly attraction. Often, these nights in the nightclubs and bars led on to parties at the great houses of the theatre directors and owners, so it was a case of mixing business with pleasure, the perfect recipe - they were to be paid for doing what they would have done anyway. One of those who frequented these parties was the wife of Erich Pommer, a highly influential producer at UFA. Thanks to this society hostess who delighted in introducing the up and coming to the influential, Marlene's name began to get known in the right circles.

Eventually, after several false starts at the casting sessions, she landed the part of a coquette in a UFA film at the Neubabelsberg studios. It was titled Manon Lescaut and directed by Arthur Robison with Lya de Putti as the female star. Marlene was to be Micheline, a pavement café provocateur who merely had to raise her head and flutter an eyelid to create a stir. Less can mean more, a lesson Marlene had learned in the experimental theatre, the Kammerspiele, where Max Reinhardt liked to stage his more progressive plays. The theatre was tiny compared to the 3,000 seat Grosses Schauspielhaus beside it, indeed the large theatre had formerly been a circus in the Berlin of Marlene's childhood when spectacle and vaudeville were the great crowd attractions before the coming of motion pictures.

On the cinema screen the smallest gesture is picked up and magnified by the camera so, just as she had in the Kammerspiele, Marlene made economy of movement her trademark. A look, a sigh, a raised finger, these were enough to signal inner power if handled with style. And in the Berlin of the 1920s if you had style you could carry anything off. People dressed the part, acted the part, nothing was as it seemed. Remarkably, the right clothes, the right manners could carry you into the inner sanctums of the rich and famous, the old barriers had disappeared with much else.

Even though Marlene had simply to play herself as the coquette in the café who becomes a nobleman's mistress, and then only for a few brief scenes, the sheer richness of the costumes and the production made the movies seem ever more desirable to her. She could dress in the most flattering and lavish dresses, although like a lot of young women she had taken to wearing men's jackets and trousers, and made her father's old monocle a virtual trademark. The Berliner Zeitung referred to the 'exceptionally pretty Marlene Dietrich' in the newspaper notices and she was getting known as a character around Berlin theatrical and cinema circles, though even she had to work at the outrageousness. The Kurfurstendamm was packed with tourists from all over Europe. They came to Berlin to see the cabaret, and go off with the tantalisingly young beautiful schoolboys and schoolgirls who hung about on the street corners ready for a brief assignation. Everything had a price in Berlin. More important, there was always someone ready to pay it.

By the beginning of 1926 the roaring sounds of the Jazz Age were ringing in Berliners' ears from America. Marlene started to carry a portable gramophone round with her to the clubs so that she could dance to the latest hits from Broadway, and later in the night at the more intimate clubs like 'Always Faithful' - for girls - she played the jazz sounds of the negro musicians who were releasing sexual innuendo into their very receptive ears. Almost without realising it, Marlene found herself becoming the breadwinner, out all night making contacts - and having an uproarious time - while Rudi, former playboy and escort to numerous beautiful actresses, had become the stay-at-home husband. But he was eager for her to progress in her career. Being seen on the social scene was an essential part of her strategy for advancement. She told Rudi about her flings with cameramen and film technicians, it was a way of learning about her chosen trade, only a complete mastery of its technicalities would allow her to establish dominance, and behind the bravura, this is what she had set her sights on. Love and career were two sides of the same existence, the film world was where she spent most of her time in one form or another, and penetrating the very layered and hierarchical system of Berlin theatre and films took immense persistence.

Marlene's first booking in 1926 was as a girl of easy virtue who could easily descend into the raffish criminal existence that was real enough outside the theatre's doors. Called *Duell am Lido* - 'Duel at the Lido' - the film was a social satire on the times. The director ordered her to wear her lesbian club outfit of trousers and jacket, with monocle. Marlene brought the mad frivolous gaiety of the bars outside to the part, and the audience immediately recognised the accuracy of the portrayal, probably thinking it exaggerated when in reality it was a pale version of what happened nightly in an arts world populated by the wealthy and criminal who liked to associate with actresses.

Then, the director Alexander Korda, who was to become a good friend, cast her as a coquette again, this time in his film *Eine du Barry von Heute - 'A Modern Du Barry'*. It was a vehicle for Korda to show off his wife Maria, but it did give Marlene the chance to dress in lavish modern dress. She loved the meticulous care that went into preparing her evening gowns covered in sequins and the glamour of the fur wraps. This world she had sensed from Grandma Felsing and she took to the style as her right and inheritance. The film's super contemporary theme was how the right dress could open doors. But it was not a great critical success. To keep the money flowing Marlene agreed to take a part in the crowd for Korda's next film, *Madame wunscht keine Kinder - 'The Lady Doesn't Want Children',* as long as he employed Rudi as his assistant. It had been months since Rudi had been able to pick up work and it was depressing him. He had won her with his aura of influence and power at the film studios, Marlene in return had to use her influence on his behalf. She did not mind at all, but he did.

After this rapid succession of films, the theatre claimed Marlene's loyalties. Briefly, in the late summer, she joined two legendary cabaret artists who were in a show called *Von Mund zu Mund' - 'From Mouth to Mouth'*. There was the husky voiced Zarah Leander, and the even more rasping voice of Claire Waldoff to accompany her in introducing the near 20 scenes in a four-hour production. Marlene also had to sing three songs, the first time she had sung on stage although she had put in good practice at the cabarets when money was tight, singing, going round bare breasted serving drinks to rich patrons, sitting on their knees, cooing in their ears, there was always a way to get the housekeeping if you were a pretty young thing, and Berlin flappers were famous throughout Europe for their lively naughty ways! The next year, 1927, Marlene recorded the songs on record. One of them, *Leben ohne Liebe*, has become a classic. Listen to it and you hear the authentic voice of Jazz Age Berlin, the seductive call of a city regretting its past and immersing itself in a hectic present to bury it for good.

Marlene felt a strong sexual attraction for Claire Waldoff, she was everything she was not: small, thick set, a schoolmistressy face, very masculine in dress with her blouses and ties. Accompanying the butchness was a tremendous sense of parody in songs like 'Willi' where she mocked the Kaiser and all this pretensions, she even included herself in these pretensions. Marlene and Claire liked to wander off arm in arm after the theatre to serenade the crowds going home, giving off a bonhomie that reflected their happiness. Marlene let Claire take her in a way she felt unable to do with a man where she much preferred to take the lead astride them, waving her arms to the skies as she rode them in Valkyrian triumph. Claire turned Marlene into a passive femme fatale, she gripped her in iron thighs and nearly squeezed the life out of her, forcing Marlene to submit to her demands for affection and tribute. Marlene found she could release her passive feminine side. But the greatest most lasting lesson she learned was not to take anything too seriously, that philosophy was not only the cornerstone of her cabaret act, it was her. She did not worry who knew about her sexual preferences, and from then on, nor did Marlene. Woman lovers represented an undemanding love, a simple exchange of affection after the complications of the man/woman relationship, where she felt she had to gratify the man's wishes in order to win them to her, for she was certainly not going to allow herself to be enslaved to any man, they had figured little in her early life as a girl, and it was not something she was going to change easily. Rudi, though he hardly approved, let Marlene have her fling with Claire, and before too long it had cooled to a mostly chaste friendship.

Soon a more demanding affair was captivating Marlene's heart, for she had very little control of where her affections - and her loins - might take her. Early in 1927, after a quick couple of comedy films produced by Ellen Richter, one of which *Kopf Hoch, Charley - 'Head up, Charley!'* - became a big box office success, she was cast in a show called 'Broadway' which featured hoodlums, clubs, jazz and chorus girls. She was cast as one of the chorus girls at the 'Paradise Club' and revelled in the opportunity to play in straight theatre a role long familiar to her from the Guildo Theilscher touring company of 12 girls, which had given her the first entrance into show business. Around this time Guildo celebrated his 50 years in the business with the party to end all parties . The hedonistic mood of Berlin was infectious. The highly successful show was transferred to Vienna, and Marlene seized the opportunity to visit the city leaving Rudi to mind the baby. A new leading man was introduced, the Austrian actor Willi Forst, who was 26, just a year older than herself. Marlene tumbled for him, he was already a well known star in Vienna and they were seen at all the fashionable night spots, arm in arm. He had humour and wit without being weighed down by German seriousness and was just the person to take Marlene even further out of herself than Claire Waldorf. A producer who saw 'Broadway' on only the second night, offered her an audition for a film he was planning, 'café Electric', with Willi Forst as the male lead. Although it was her first female lead, Marlene took great care to feign indifference to his offer especially as there was to be a film test that Sascha Film, a subsidiary of UFA, insisted upon. Even though the film test, where Willi and Marlene played a love scene with great conviction, was not regarded as sufficiently good, Willi insisted that Marlene play the part of the spoilt rich businessman's daughter who he seduces in the Café Electric with his gigolo ways. The Austrian star got his way and Marlene her first lead. As they shot the love scenes for real and repeated them, the heat between the couple was there for all the world to see on camera. Rudi arrived in Vienna as talk of the romance found its way into the flourishing gossip columns that talked of nothing but the lives of the glamorous new film stars seen to live in a different universe from the man in the street. Rudi issued an ultimatum. Either Marlene stopped the romance with Willi or he would end the marriage. Marlene was briefly stunned. Then he announced he had a long term girlfriend, Tamara Matul, a Russian dancer, who he would move into the family apartment if Marlene did not agree. Never one to compromise, Marlene let him move Tamara in. She would, she guessed, provide more of a mother figure for little Maria than she was able to do faraway in Vienna.

The taste of stardom and being the talk of the gossip columns in Vienna was sweet. *'Broadway'* had launched Marlene in Berlin society, helped by a little number where she cycled her legs on stage under the searching brightness of the theatre spotlights, the sensational routine was straight from Marlene's training routine in the men's gyms. It had a stunning effect on the theatre audiences. Her long perfect legs became the talk of first Berlin and then Vienna. One evening she received a request from the Sascha film company. Count Kolowrat, the owner, was dying from cancer, he wanted her to grace his bedroom to flash her legs before him as his dying wish. He was a gargantuan man who weighed some 360 pounds. Marlene dutifully appeared in his bedroom and surveyed the tragic fate of the man, bedridden and not long for this world. With a smile and whirl she went through her routine, flashing her legs and naked thighs before him. With a dismissive wave the poor creature indicated he had had enough. But the incident was talked about. Count Kolowrat was a partner of Alfred Hugenburg who owned the UFA film studios. In 1928 upon Marlene's eventual return to Berlin she received an equally strange request from Alfred Hugenburg. Would she attend the opera after a dinner at the Olympus Club in Berlin where he had a very important guest he wished to entertain and impress? She naturally complied, taking along Carl Zuckmayer, a writer who had sympathies for a National Socialist party that was causing waves in Bavaria. The guest of the evening was Adolf Hitler, the leader of the National Socialists. Hugenburg, who had great wealth and influence, was prepared to deal with the Nazis as part of his campaign to restore the old conservative German values. He wanted Hitler to sign a pact of co-operation with him, in return he would give the Nazis prominent coverage in his newspapers.

Marlene never spoke of her meeting with the 'horrible little Austrian dwarf' but even her description speaks of some knowledge of his physical presence. He seemed to drain women he came in contact with and produce a mixed fascination and horror. Two of the few people alive who can confirm this personal contact between the future Hollywood star and the dictator are Leni Riefenstahl and Billy Wilder.

Perhaps indicating her still smouldering resentment Leni Riefenstahl denies that she and Marlene were ever friends claiming they only met two or three times whereas in fact they used to frequent the same cafés in the Kurfurstendam on a regular basis besides working in the same studios and socialising in the tightly knit film crowd circles. While Billy Wilder when casting Marlene in a later film as a German with a past who meets Nazis at the opera (he can hardly resist basing his films on real life incidents) preferred to write his own story of the encounter, but never did before his recent death.

Hitler was charm itself at the opera. It had been his greatest treat when poor and living on a small orphan's pension in Vienna in the period between 1907 and 1913. His attempts to gain an entrance to the Art Academy had confirmed him in his rage at the Jewish conspiracy that robbed him of recognition for his artistic skills and he had had to survive by painting tourist postcards and pictures sold to Jewish dealers. But gratitude for this help when he was down on his luck were conspicuously absent from a man badly damaged in his emotional responses from early youth. The strict old customs official and his much younger wife between them set up a marked need in the oldest surviving son to both rebel against authority and grovel before sadistic punishment when his father was around and then to bathe in his mother's unquestioning love when the father was absent. Ever after he sought this adoration, first from a specific woman and then from a nation as Germany became his great love.

There was a sinister air to the club in the presence of this drab small Austrian. Marlene found herself both repulsed to gaze upon him and yet drawn back again and again to the dark pits of his eyes. They had a mesmeric quality, no light emitted from the pupils, there was only darkness. He was charming enough that evening, trying to laugh and smile, but she sensed the absolute control he exerted over himself, and his control over everyone else, he appeared to be able to make everyone dance to his tune, to orchestrate them like puppets, it was as if he were the only person truly alive in the room, everyone else seemed false in comparison to this man who burned with a fierce primitive energy. Hugenburg knew Hitler liked to be seen in the company of beautiful women, which was why he had invited his top actresses to be present for the evening. Hitler acknowledged Marlene with the ghost of a smile, when she was introduced at his table and then he got back to his true passion, the political business. All night long she watched as he dominated everyone there by his presence, hardly moving, nodding occasionally, affecting the dapper ways of a man of influence, even though they all knew his power came from his storm troopers who ferociously attacked any who dared oppose them, so savage were the beatings that people often died under the bullying blows from feet, iron bars and knives. It had been the preferred tactic on the streets of Munich where he had tried to seize power five years before, on that occasion the state forces had been too strong for his few followers but though still small his party was growing in numbers in the conservative south of Germany. Marlene left the club that evening with a deep sense of foreboding about what would happen to Germany with Hugenburg and Hitler in league together.

Three years later she heard how Hitler's niece, Geli Rabaul, had committed suicide after being humiliated sexually. There were rumours it was Hitler who had pushed her to these extremes. The talk was of how he had liked to draw Geli wide open in graphic detail, and these pictures had found their way into the hands of a blackmailer. It was also said that his sexual tastes included Geli crouching over his face while he studied her genitals and grovelled beneath protesting his worthlessness with the climax achieved by him demanding she urinate over him. Later still Marlene remembered this story when yet another of the women Hitler had known intimately committed suicide. This time it was Renate Muller, another actress, who reported that she had been invited to the Chancellery for the night to gratify the Chancellor's pleasure. After she removed her clothes he started grovelling on the floor at her feet and demanding she kick and humiliate him, all the time feverishly denouncing his baseness and worthlessness. Terror was added to the proceedings by his sexual overtures commencing with a description of Gestapo torture methods. Marlene remembered Hitler's wish for the showgirls in the club to parade their bottoms before him as though about to be buggered. The man was a pervert, nothing was beyond him, she had known that immediately, well before he had the opportunity to play out his obscene obsessions before a wider audience. To the Berliners he was a provincial who could be safely played along, Hugenburg promised the former corporal a handsome financial support in return for Hitler's backing of his aims.

But the formative years in Vienna stayed with Hitler, even more than in Berlin there was a fetid doomed atmosphere there in the days leading up to the First World War. He had absorbed all this explosive and fated decay as the Habsburg Empire tottered towards its end, an end Hitler had predicted and which had fatally infected him as well as it had infected artists like Gustav Mahler and Klimt, while Freud probed the psyche of Vienna and found sex and death irretrievably mixed in the souls of the Viennese. It was the same atmosphere that von Sternberg himself had absorbed in his early years. Now was to come a film that depicted as never before the attractions and entrapments of this extreme sado-masochistic view of life. By the time it was over the whole world would be exposed to such a view of human relationships. The depictors were to be Josef von Sternberg and Marlene Dietrich playing out in life and on film a relationship heavily tinged with both masochism and sadism in a heady intoxicating brew made possible by the dream machine of the modern cinema

Chapter Five

The casting of *The Blue Angel*

Es liegt in der Luft - 'It's in the Air' - could have described the Berlin of 1928, anything seemed possible. It was actually the name of a stage play with Margo Lion in the lead role and Marlene Dietrich as her accompanying star. It caused a stir, even in those heady days, for its portrayal of Margo and herself as bosom buddies singing a song suggestive of girlish intimacies. It was chic to be fresh with the ladies, and Marlene wore a bouquet of violets - emblematic of lesbian love - to raise some more eyebrows among the audience.

Her next project was a film - *Prinzessin Olala* - where, with her red gold hair lightened to Scandinavian blonde, the press started to comment on her similarities to Garbo. Naturally, they derided this attempt to imitate the young Swedish girl who by now had become a legend in America. The hunt was on to find someone who could rival her audience-pulling power in the cinema. In this year she made a film with John Gilbert which brought many more fans under her sway, women in particular were won over by her strangely passive yet totally expressive face, looks and limpid actions. There was gossip of the lovers on screen being lovers in real life, which turned out to be true enough, Gilbert had managed to open the legs of the frigid Scandinavian was how Marlene retold the story in the pavement cafés.

The next film, *Die Frau nach der man sich sehnt* - 'The Woman One Longs For' - called forth even more Garbo comparisons. One film magazine even produced a front cover with half of it showing Garbo, and the other half Marlene. The brooding creature the two halves created did have a powerful presence and existence of its own. People began to talk and speculate about Germany's challenge to Sweden. The film scouts, who the big American studios like Paramount and

Universal kept in Berlin, sent telegrams off to Hollywood noting the fact that there was another Garbo in the making. 'This is the new kind of woman,' said one of the Berlin film critics. After years of effort, Marlene was beginning to be noticed, but she had had too many disappointments and setbacks in the film world to expect overnight success. To aid her chances she had a nose cosmetic surgery job in the summer to lessen the width of the nostrils, which seemed to her very unGerman and quite Slavic, with an annoying turned up end. The features were smoothed into a closer approximation to the film world's idea of a femme fatale and the German peasant earthiness of her mother's ancestors was hidden from sight. The operation, quite unusual in those days, was a success. Early September found Marlene back in the theatre playing a millionaire's girlfriend in *Twei Kravaten - 'Two Neckties'* - a wicked Berlin send-up of the American (and German) good life with its displays of wealth and over-consumption.

After her experiences in the war and its aftermath, all waste offended Marlene, she entered into the comedy's mocking ways with gusto, although she had, not unusually, just one line, as well as a part where she looked out from a luxury liner's deck rail while the wind machine blew the loose skirt she was wearing closely about her upper limbs and flat stomach, her most beguiling features. A few days after the show opened to hugely successful critical acclaim there was a man in the audience who was to change her way of life forever, but at the time she was unaware of his presence. He had come to check out two other players who he had just signed for the film he was planning, Germany's first all-talking picture. Marlene had heard the rumours that this was going to be a big film, speculation was rife in the theatrical night spots about who might win the lead. The hot favourite appeared to be Lucie Mannheim, but she was a very cultured lady, and Marlene heard the part called for the actress to play a cheap floosie in a working men's nightclub. Next Marlene heard Emil Jannings was to play the lead role. He had progressed over the years from when had been in *'The Tragedy of Love'* and Rudi had given Marlene her first real role as the judge's mischievous little coquette. Marlene began to wildly speculate that perhaps she could use this distant link with Jannings to get considered for the part. He later claimed to have recommended her to Josef von Sternberg, the man who had come anonymously to the theatre to see her skirts being blown around her body. Her name was mentioned early for the part by the UFA studio executives, including Erich Pommer, the film's producer, but there was no agreement and von Sternberg insisted on continuing the search. The American director had heard of the existence of a German Garbo, and was looking for this dream woman, a woman he could mould into his fantasies of seduction and entrapment just as the Swedish-based-director Mauritz Stiller had with Greta Garbo.

Rumours continued to buzz around town as the search continued. Trude Hesterberg was the new favourite but she was too well known to play the part of a tart, it was not her style. Marlene knew her coquette image from so many films must stand her in some good stead. But when von Sternberg had come to see Hans Albers and Road Valetti perform in the theatre, he could hardly have known that the ethereal beauty he saw gazing distantly into the audience with a look of enchantment and seduction upon her otherwise vacant mind was merely blissfully happy to be in the presence of her lover, for Hans Albers and Marlene were at the beginning of a passionate affair that could not help but bring a glow to her face, he was the most proficient lover yet, a mature man who quickly won the adoration of a still rather naive young girl. And this in spite of the all night revelries at which she made her presence felt. Getting known in the right circles was a full-time job for her, she was determined to make the breakthrough, but it never arrived. An invitation to an audition in front of the great American director arrived the day after his visit to the theatre.

Marlene sensed this was to be no ordinary audition. Rudi also sensed the import of the call and haughtily insisted there was no need for a film test. He was sure Marlene would use the occasion to seduce von Sternberg and win the part. The still married couple's physical love life had petered out to only the occasional encounter, he had become more her friend and business adviser, while Maria was more used to having Rudi's girlfriend Tamara with her in the evenings than Marlene, work as always had to take precedence. She was sure the film audition and test would lead to disappointment and tried not to build up her hopes. At the same time she prepared for the audition with unusual care even for someone who looked on each public outing as an acting part.

There were three people present at the audition, Rudi's feared seduction scene could not be played out. Besides von Sternberg, there was Erich Pommer, the film's UFA producer, and Emil Jannings, the star of the film. Jannings had invited von Sternberg to the theatre the previous evening and had mentioned he should look out for Marlene. It was also he who had insisted von Sternberg be brought over for his first German talkie, after he had worked successfully with director the previous year in Hollywood on his film 'The Way of All Flesh'. It had been a big hit and Jannings lorded over creation as the most famous actor in the world, with his fee for the new film set at the fabulous sum of $200,000. When Marlene's name had come up at the film studio early on, it was Pommer, not Jannings, who had objected. 'Not that whore,' were his reported words. It was not clear if he was referring to her chequered private life, or to the endless succession of coquettes on the edge of the demi-monde she portrayed on film, there was a thin line in any case between the two characters.

Marlene spent all morning dressing for the audition. She sought to look like a very correct married woman, in grey long dress, with gloves, and a suitably modest expression, anxious to repress any hints of subterranean passions in her character which would worry the all-powerful American director. The three men, lounging in their chairs, asked her to walk around the room. Von Sternberg, nervous and intense, quickly got up and came over to Marlene after she had finished her slow walk.

'Your dress is too loose,' he said abruptly and began pinning back the folds until it clung to her body, which he continuously brushed against. Marlene was excited by this bodily contact, and so, she could tell, was he. She gave him a knowing look each time he brushed against her, but Jannings and Pommer thought little of the diminutive American's interest in the actress's dress, the atmosphere of the audition was very correct.

'Thank you, Fraulein Dietrich', said Pommer tersely as the audition closed.

'I would like you to do a film test tomorrow,' von Sternberg said softly and urgently , as he took Marlene's arm and ushered her out the room. Once outside, he also suggested she call him at his hotel on the Kurfurstendamm.

He went back into the room and canvassed the views of both Jannings and Pommer who proved adamantly opposed to his hiring her for the female lead. Jannings followed Pommer's estimation of the young actress, but von Sternberg insisted that a film test be made, threatening to return to America if he could not have his way. Both Jannings and Pommer retreated and the next day, after a night when Marlene indulged von Sternberg's every whim, all of a sadistic nature, she returned for a film test.

Von Sternberg had arranged for a piano to be on the set, and asked Marlene to sing a song. She had not brought any sheet music to give the pianist, Friedrich Hollander, who had also been in 'The Tragedy of Love' all those years ago.

'Don't worry, just sing a song you know,' said von Sternberg who she sensed to be on her side, even though she had had to wait much of the day while Lucie Mannheim was tested, with special close-ups of her behind for Jannings' delectation, she had a large rear, and this was how the big broad German liked his women.

Marlene sang a current song from the Berlin café scene whose main theme was:

61

*'Why get upset when an affair comes to an end,
When there is another waiting round the corner?'*

She could see von Sternberg liked the sentiments of cynical slick Berlin society, it tuned in with something in his own character.

'Sit on the piano now, roll down a stocking,' he commanded.

She struggled on to the piano in her tight sequined dress, having spent ages pulling herself into it that day, and having laboriously teased every wave of hair into position in the dressing rooms.

'Do you know *'You're the Cream in my Coffee'*?' she asked Friedrich.

'No,' he said apologetically, anxious to help.

'Alright, I'll sing the first couple of lines, you'll get the hang of it.'

It was a song from one of the new Broadway musicals.

'Stop,' cried von Sternberg, 'that's it, I want to film that, with you talking to the pianist, just like that.'

Marlene did not pretend to understand why the American director wanted her to repeat the question in the nonchalent off-hand manner she had just used, the low key remark had none of the drama of the movies in its enunciation. That was what von Sternberg found so exciting.

After the film test there followed a long period while Marlene awaited confirmation she had won the part. She began showing von Sternberg some of the more exotic spots of Berlin's nightlife, sometimes in the company of his wife Riza and her husband Rudi. Von Sternberg told her of the battles he was having with UFA. They hated the film test, insisted on Lucie Mannheim, but she had her supporters, one of the film's scriptwriters was on her side. Carl Zuckmayer was a poet and playwright who von Sternberg was using to rewrite a book by Heinrich Mann called *Professor Umraut* - *'Professor Crap'* is the nearest English translation. Carl also became Marlene's lover as she pursued the elusive film part. Heinrich Mann forecast that the success of the film would depend on the attraction of her naked thighs, while Jannings declared her sex appeal would divert attention from his starring role. Von Sternberg threatened to return to the USA unless UFA capitulated to his commands. Each night in his room Marlene stoked his passion for the encounters in the morning. Alfred Hugenburg, UFA's owner, became involved. He hated the film's story of the downfall of a good German teacher, his Nationalist Party were fervid conservatives who in theory supported all the old German values of family and discipline. But von Sternberg held the upper hand, he was Paramount's representative and UFA desperately wanted to break into the American market. The film was going to be recorded in English and German simultaneously, and von Sternberg was vital for this dual soundtrack, on a technical level as well, for only he of all the technicians had worked with sound throughout a complete film, the only German movies with sound had simply had musical interludes on the otherwise silent soundtracks.

All the negotiations came to a head. Erich Pommer continued to say 'No' after the film test results, Jannings veered towards Lucie Mannheim. Von Sternberg imperiously declared,

'You have just confirmed that I was right. Marlene Dietrich is perfect for this role.'

He had already caught on film the tramp of a bar girl oozing her languid bored attractions in the late night clubs. It shocked the snobby Berliner film makers who preferred their glamorous balls and social dinners. The woman von Sternberg wanted was a real low-life character, and he thought he had found her. As Marlene was to discover, this was actually the background of the American director. He had grown up in the slums of pre-war Vienna where he ran around with the street urchins. His family lived right in the heart of the city's red light district where young women from all over the old Habsburg Empire came in search of some money, any money, anyhow. He had observed these street girls close up and knew their ways intimately from a very early age. He would tell her of the little games they would play where they would ran up behind the prostitutes hanging around on street corners and pulled up their skirts to shame them by exposing their private parts. All around him were the poor of the great sprawling polyglot empire struggling to make a living, as was his own family. At the age of 7 he was shipped across the Atlantic to join his father who had gone on ahead to seek a living in the USA, but they lived in slums just as bad thrown into a great mass of immigrants fleeing pogroms of Jews in imperial Russia. At the age of 10 he and his mother, sisters and brother were returned to Vienna until when he was 14 once again the call came for them to join their absent father in America who had at last established a toehold on the great continent. By this time the young adolescent had seen at first hand just what depravities were forced on the Viennese poor. Privacy was non-existent, there were thousands of homeless, people living in doorways and parks, even in the sewers. Beds were rented out for the night as long as the occupants left in the morning in the hopelessly crowded rooms where three and four people shared a floor or a bed. For the really poor there were the flop houses where up to twenty people would crowd in, every last inch taken, the two sexes mixed irretrievably amongst the dirt and the squalor while women earned themselves enough to eat the next day by sleeping with a succession of men throughout the night. There was little further to go down when you hit bottom in Vienna. And Jonas had seen all these sights for himself. On his return to America he put his street wisdom into practice.

Jonas was expected to fend for himself and got into movies quite by chance. One day he was with some friends in New York City's Central Park sheltering from a rain storm when some girls joined them as lightning flashed overhead. The girls took them back to their parents' house where the father made a living restoring old film reels that had become battered from their frequent use in the picture palaces which were springing up in the early 1910s. Jonas Sternberg progressed from film doctor to processor of films through a very practical apprenticeship that saw him master all the technicalities (and possibilities) of early film. His visual education was the fine art galleries and museums of New York, which were richly endowed by the great American monopoly capitalists like Carnegie and Rockefeller who had made fortunes of astounding sizes from their stranglehold on the steel, railway and shipping industries. Eventually von Sternberg had gone to Hollywood as the mainly East European Jewish migrants who formed the heart of the new film industry went west to film in the marvellous light of southern California in a small village called Hollywood on the outskirts of Los Angeles - City of the Angels. Charlie Chaplin took a huge gamble by letting him make a film which featured one of the young women he was currently besotted with. Like Sternberg, he too was from the slums and obsessed by young women. It was the secret link. He added the aristocratic 'von' to his name and became Joseph rather than Jonas. The 'von' affectation was copied from the early German film director genius, von Stroheim. Sternberg's film about the American gangster underworld of the late 1920s showed, with unusual realism, the brutality of their lives. Paramount gave him their backing on the strength of two box office hits among some more well-regarded but commercial failures. When Jannings had invited him to Europe, he had already heard the reported rumours of a new Garbo and wanted to become like Mauritz Stiller, the discoverer of a film icon.

This background helps to explain the appeal of Professor Umraut, which was written in 1905 by Heinrich Mann. It is the story of how a morally upright schoolteacher takes his adolescent pupils to task for having pictures of 'Lola Lola', as von Sternberg named her, a cabaret performer in a poor working class district of Lubeck. He then follows them to a performance and is smitten by the charms she sends his way. A night with Lola Lola and the professor abandons bourgeois respectability for the arms of his beloved. She is not accepted by the school and the professor is dismissed after a sterling 25 years service. He becomes Lola Lola's manager (or pimp) and then her assistant. Finally he is reduced to the role of a clown, who has rotten eggs smashed on his skull by the irrepressible Lola Lola as part of the act. In the book, the disgraced professor gets his revenge by tempting the local worthies, including his persecutors, into his club and blackmailing them with details of their pernicious passions for under-age schoolgirls and worse. So the book gives the professor a revenge of sorts. This had no appeal for von Sternberg who was attracted by the entrapment and degrading of the schoolmaster, representative of the old repressive values which had once held him in poverty. Above all, he sought to make actual his vision of a woman who, almost in spite of herself, acts as the rock upon which male desires will founder and result in ultimate debasement. Von Sternberg wished to explore this masochistic coarsening to its very end, to revel in the depths to which the schoolmaster would sink. There can be no doubt it was a semi-autobiographical depiction. The strutting emperor of the stage turned in bed into a pathetic weak man, he was 5'4", who wished to be gradually humiliated. Marlene acted as his living doll who he first wakened to life and then was consumed by her. Their love sessions always finished this way with her in total control while he enjoyed his enslavement. But these chinks in his armour are what gave Jonas Sternberg, Jewish poor boy from Vienna, his strengths as Josef von Sternberg, Hollywood director and tyrant, observer and recorder of all human foibles and weakness. The couple had begun a relationship in which one sought to dominate and humiliate the other, on set and off. All their films were but a description of this obsessive love that was to be written across the screens of the world.

The filming of *The Blue Angel*, simultaneously recorded in German and English, began on 4 November, 1929, a week after Wall Street had suffered an unprecedented drop in its stock prices. Marlene Dietrich was paid $5,000 for her hard-won part as Lola Lola.

Chapter Six

The filming of *The Blue Angel*

Marlene Dietrich was convinced *'The Blue Angel'* would finish her career, not make it. So were the executives from UFA, who declined to take up an option in the contract giving them first choice ahead of von Sternberg in using her for her next film. *'The Blue Angel'* deals with the murkier aspects of human existence, as is immediately flagged in the setting so brilliantly captured by the film's director. Von Sternberg lovingly recreated the winding lanes of the poor part of a mediaeval town, basing his expert portrayal on the poverty-plagued streets he had known intimately in Vienna. The setting is in Lübeck as for the book, but it is quite definitely the old sailors' part of town, where the ships of the Hanseatic League had docked as trade propelled Lübeck to pre-eminence in mediaeval times. But those glory days had faded well before the Kaiser's War which was to lay Germany so low. The seeds of decay were brought into focus by von Sternberg, there was no detail too small for him, he was always the first on the set, well before the janitors and the actors who all arrived promptly at seven in the morning to begin their make-up.

He had to shoot all the scenes first in German and then in English, although some in the English version of the film are left in German where they involve minor characters. Von Sternberg was allowed to create an astonishingly realistic film by Hollywood standards. The studio bosses did not know he was creating the old corrupt Europe he knew so well rather than a tinsel town fabrication.

The film opens beautifully with the teacher, Emil Jannings, in his classroom, while echoing footsteps are heard, before cutting to a cleaning lady throwing some water over a poster advertising the performances of 'Lola Lola' at *The Blue Angel'* cabaret bar. On the poster a small angel clings to Lola Lola's leg, which is long and elegant. Her torso is barely covered by a tight fitting garment. It is more daring than the outfit Marlene wore in the film, for people still emerging from the stiff public morality of the German imperial heyday, it was distinctly shocking. Von Sternberg knew exactly how far he could go, and in Lola Lola he wished to create his own ideal of the sexually provocative woman who had learnt her trade the hard way on the streets. Von Sternberg claimed he merely revealed what was already there in Marlene Dietrich, he had immediately spotted the insouciance of the true Berliner, hard to shock and hard to outwit. From the very beginning they were lovers off the screen, and this allowed her to sit with him until late into the night as he looked at the day's rushes and prepared himself for the next morning's shoot. When he scanned through the reels, frame by frame, she became aware of a master craftsman at work, every shot was perfectly framed, perfectly lit, even the sound quality has another dimension to it in setting the mood, indeed he appreciated more of its emotional qualities than many later directors who supplied the emotive quality from background music.

In *'The Blue Angel'*, every sense is called into play, here von Sternberg had learnt from the old High German expressionist cinema which created film from the play of light and dark, so that a whole world is summoned up, rather than just an action depicted. The loving attention to detail means that the film even today retains its extraordinary vivid quality while the players are immensely believable. All this is the work of von Sternberg alone, who demanded and got the absolute right to dictate how each set looked and was lit. The sound had to be right at the time the film was shot, there was no facility for adding the soundtrack later in a dub, but all these technical details were mastered completely by a man who had learnt his trade so painstakingly restoring each frame of a film by hand, he knew more about each technical function than even the alleged technicians.

Filming followed a set pattern, it was just like going to work at an office. From 7am the actors prepared their make-up ready for action at 9am. However, it was rare for this to go altogether smoothly. Jannings was an actor who could only deliver his performance after he had suitably raised his emotional temperature, and on '*The Blue Angel*' Marlene had the chance to see at first hand exactly what this entailed. If von Sternberg made the fatal mistake of not enquiring after Emil's health, the word would come from his dressing room that he was mortally unwell and would not be able to perform. Von Sternberg would then visit Jannings in his dressing room where he sat facing the mirror, a quivering mass of jellified fear who could not face the performance he was due to give. Only von Sternberg's entreaties and frequent reassurances that he was indeed the greatest actor in the world persuaded him to venture out, when he would give a superlative performance. In the early days of the shoot, he was playing the bombastic, bullying schoolmaster who was precise in his routine, sitting there imperiously waiting to be served his breakfast by his landlady and then fastidiously checking his handkerchief is in place in his top pocket before venturing out to rule his pupils, aged from 16-18, with a rod of iron. It is in one of these lessons that he comes across a picture of Lola Lola for the first time, the onlooker is required to blow up the skirts of Lola Lola to reveal her long legs. Soon he discovers more pictures of the cabaret artist and is determined to follow his charges to see what manner of woman it is who has them in her grasp. All this part of the film Jannings managed with superb aplomb, but for the actor and for the character it is a descent into hell. First, he has to defend Lola Lola against the demands of a sea captain who delivers a champagne bottle to her dressing room and believes this is enough to purchase her for the night. At the time the film was set, 1924, this would indeed have been the case for many a cabaret artiste taking her chances in the inflation-ruined country. Professor Umraut sees the captain off with a bellowing denunciation and a firm fist. He wins over Lola Lola's grudging admiration while he is rewarded with a glimpse from the bottom of a spiral staircase of her vagina as she tosses down her French cami knickers to him. All this is perfectly registered on Jannings' face, the shock turning to intrigue turning to reluctant but heartfelt pursuit of the delicious fruit he has not tasted in his very ordered life.

For the ultimate seduction of the professor, von Sternberg had ordered Friedrich Hollander to compose a song, which, with his knowledge of the Berlin cabaret scene, perfectly matches the mood of the early 1920s. In literal English translation it says,

'I am from top to toe built for love
that's the way I am
that's my whole purpose'

In the even more cool English lyrics this is reworked as:

'Falling in love again, what am I to do
Never wanted to, I can't help it.'

The performance was wrung from Marlene by a director who was obsessive on the phrasing, the looks to be cast at the professor, the suggestive raising of the legs to reveal pale thighs shrouded in frilly knickers. Throughout most of the film he had one of the four cameras trained on Marlene's pelvis, precisely the angle of one of the most famous shots in the film lexicon where Marlene sits on a barrel revealing her charms. She has transported herself back to the world she knew so well of the cabaret clubs, eyeing up a likely customer for the night, evaluating and inviting the pick of the evening's audience, who for the purposes of the film is to be the shy but melting school professor.

At one point von Sternberg shouted in a mock exasperated voice, 'Adjust your knickers, we can see your pubic hair, you filthy sow.' Marlene laughed. Leni Riefestahl, who was on set that day and had been in the running for the part, remembers it being less pungent a comment, but there was a distinctly coarse side to von Sternberg even on the film set.

After 200 takes, no less, the song was committed to film and von Sternberg finally moved on, but for Marlene her career was forever haunted by this near perfect evocation of the Berlin cabaret atmosphere of the mid 20s, and who knew that better than her? She had been a chorus girl for 7 years and only the previous year had she finally stopped dancing and flashing her legs for a living when the film and stage work was not plentiful, as happened often. Film shoots lasted a few weeks, and usually she appeared in one or two scenes at most. The pay was normally in the range of 50 to 100 marks, little more than a shop girl's monthly wage. The actors and actresses were expected to make up for this with the perks of the jobs at parties and private gatherings. Marlene lived for the shows, they were her life, on top of which she was increasingly the one who kept the household together, Rudi's career had never really progressed from those first early days of promise.

The atmosphere of the film set subtly changed after the professor proposed to Lola Lola and she, laughing a hard-bitten Berlin street girl laugh, accepted. In the film the professor is dismissed from the school by the headmaster when the boys mock his obsession with Lola Lola through their explicit drawings on the blackboard. In the early morning make-up sessions, Jannings developed the obsessions of someone who demands to be punished. One day he fell to the floor in a nervous state of exhaustion after saying he could not possibly go on with 'that tart' again. He was by now insanely jealous of her 'lunches' when von Sternberg and she would retire to a hotel to enact for themselves the grand passion that can spark between man and woman, it was a mood to perfectly match the obsessions depicted on the film. But Emil was determined not to be upstaged.

He wanted von Sternberg to lunch with him, to keep Marlene out of the director's favoured regard.

'What can a woman give you, that I can't?' he pitifully demanded of von Sternberg. 'Don't I offer you my soul, my body, in every performance. Punish me if it is not good enough, here whip me, whip me I say for not being the actor who matches your demands.'

Von Sternberg obediently whipped Jannings and Jannings returned to the sound set purged of all hate for the dictatorial director, who never handed out praise but merely put the performers through their motions again and again and again till it matched what he had in his mind and would never reveal to the actors. They were merely puppets in his eyes, there to follow his instructions to the letter. This Marlene knew and obediently followed, realising it was how she would progress in her own acting career. Von Sternberg had seen how the best of Hollywood films were directed and it was a new experience for Marlene to witness this fanatical attention to every detail, with a vision imposed on the chaotic scenes from high above. The actors never had the whole picture and would have to wait for the film itself to unravel the full message he was seeking to capture on celluloid.

Marlene was aware from the details von Sternberg worked into every scene that he was determined *The Blue Angel* cabaret bar was to be seen as a decadent low-life bar with no redeeming features. A sad faced clown surveys the professor on each visit and gives a perfect depiction of the vanity of all human wishes with his wan, sad but still curious face as he sees the fate of another unfortunate unfolding. Bears are tugged past the fat and ageing performer's dressing room by bit-part players, seedy magicians well past their prime come in and out of Lola Lola's room, all around is an air of depravity with no turning back, this is the end of all hopes the film clearly says in a stunningly realistic portrayal of the mood of those times. It is 'Joyless Street' again, where only the besmirching of innocence gives true pleasure to the players, and Lola Lola cannot help but be the instrument of downfall for all that the old Germany stood for, so well portrayed in the stout frame and certainties of Professor Umraut.

Marlene quickly realised that Josef von Sternberg saw another cuckolding in the story. Just as the years flash by from the marriage of 1925 to the present day of 1929 in the film, so her own married life flashed by. For Marlene and for von Sternberg, there was an element of Rudi in the professor's fate, forced by circumstance to become her clown-like assistant after he is unable to work in his own calling. Nemesis comes in the film when the manager of the cabaret insists they are to return to his hometown of Lubeck to perform. The professor will hear none of it but is forced to realise he has no choice, he has become a camp follower of the seedy show. He is forced on stage after having been announced as the former professor from the local high school. As he stands there in front of the mocking crowd, he catches a glimpse of Lola Lola in the arms of the leading man and realises he has lost her as a rotten egg is smashed over his skull and he is meant to give a *'cock a doddle do'* crow. In a stunning acting performance, Jannings conveys all the shame and ridicule heaped upon his great frame, the whippings and pleadings in his dressing room allowed him to reach this demonic stage of utter desolation. In the film a new Marlene Dietrich is unveiled, for as life once again mirrors art, she maintained her affair with Hans Albers at the same time as the new one with von Sternberg had commenced. No man, even a film director, was going to own her. Von Sternberg saw his own cuckolding and faithfully captured it on film. The only part of The Blue Angel where Marlene's acting fails, is the look of shock on her face when she is discovered in the arms of the leading man. The old hyperbole of the silent films is sketched on her features, it is unbelievable, not least because she always expected her men to realise that because they had loved her, it did not in any way mean that they owned me. She was always and forever determined to be a free agent, ready to give the blessings of her physical love to whoever she thought so deserved, for her love had a universal yet strangely impersonal character, an emotion to be used to calm the world and refresh its eyes when they became downcast.

This she had learnt at high cost on the streets of Berlin in the early 20s, soon it was a lesson she could usefully apply to rest of the world as the first hints of renewed depression and recession began to be hinted at in the beginning months of

1930. By mid February the film was complete, although von Sternberg would let no one see it until the premier on March 30.

As soon as the film was cut to von Sternberg's satisfaction he had returned to America, with the promise that he would arrange a film contract with Paramount for Marlene , since he was absolutely certain that the film would be a major success. She was far less certain, and noted that the UFA executives declined to take up their option on seeing the preview von Sternberg arranged for Erich Pommer, the producer, and his bosses. Finally the cable came through from Hollywood, she had a contract and began preparations for departing to America. She explained to Rudi and Maria that she would go on ahead, that the first film could easily be a disaster, and there was no point in uprooting their lives with this failure in prospect. At the same time she was determined to leave Berlin on a high note.

At the first showing of the film, the day before the official premiere, neither she nor Emil Jannings were allowed to be present. Jannings had a presentiment that all was not well for his career. He had told von Sternberg that he never wished to work with him or see him ever again, even though he said, 'I will weep on hearing of your death, and you will weep on hearing of mine.' With that he had scuttled out of von Sternberg's office, difficult to the last. They certainly never did meet again, though with the benefit of the years it is possible to appreciate that this was Emil Jannings' finest performance, he captured the wretched professor and his fate perfectly. That it found a deep resonance within his own tortured self had much to do with this fine acting performance.

By the time of the premiere Marlene still did not know whether she had a hit or a flop on her hands, she could not imagine why Germany or, even more, America, should be emotionally involved in the fate of one of the many cabaret girls who could be found in every sleazy bar in either country. But she prepared for the premiere as though it were a film set, dressed in a sequinned body-hugging dress. As the lights went down she pressed up to the glass in the viewing room at the back of the cinema where they could see the reaction of the audience (in those days people reacted to film rather like they still do to theatre). Emil Jannings affected a nonchalant lack of concern at the reaction of the public, even turning his back on the screen to natter about anything but the film to his cronies, after all he was the most famous actor in the world. By the time the film reached the first scenes where Lola Lola is depicted in action in '*The Blue Angel*' Marlene became aware of a buzz in the audience. Their hearts were warming to this sailor's girl with her Low German accent, her casual acceptance of her role as a temptress. By the time of the film's end, with Lola Lola sitting astride a chair singing defiantly to the audience of *'Falling in Love Again'*, she had become a new person, a star, both on screen and in her own estimation. The audience applause was deafening and rolled on and on as she made her way towards the exit for a car which Willi Forsch had laid on. Clutching champagne glasses and luggage they fell about in the back as it roared off into the night, throwing their glasses out behind onto the road. Willi hugged Marlene, delighted for her success, and she showered him with kisses, all too aware that the stardom she had long sought now finally beckoned. They caught the boat train with seconds to spare, indeed the train's departure was delayed until her arrival. She was not to know that it would be long months before she would return again to Berlin, and in a sense she never really came back at all.

Chapter Seven

Arrival in Hollywood

Before the age of planes, it was a real adventure to travel to America, it took five days for the ship to make its way against the strong headwinds into New York's harbour. Marlene's dear friend Resi accompanied her, but she was seasick for most of the voyage, while Marlene stayed largely in the cabin rather than venture out among the passengers. Even a boat trip was a public performance as far as she was concerned, the elusive allure of the film star had to be projected. However, she did not allow for the remarkable friendliness of the Americans, a couple from New York who ran a clothing store befriended her, they were Jimmy and Bianca Brooks. Later, she was to shop at Jimmy's store to buy her men's evening dresswear, which she used as a trademark in easily shockable America. Jimmy and Marlene got on famously, while she had great fun shocking his wife by flicking through the pages of one of her Berlin books where women kissed and fondled one another with varying degrees of intimacy. Bianca was quite scandalised, Marlene told her this was considered sophisticated behaviour in Berlin and Paris. Marlene never did get used to American prudery and fascination with sexual scandal. Or American men's forwardness and lack of gallantry.

She had a taste of this on her first night in New York. After arrival, when she was told to dress in mink even though it was 10 o'clock in the morning in order to fulfill the expectations of the reporters and photographers about what a glamorous European movie star should look like, she spent much of the day searching for a dentist who could take care of Resi's aching teeth. The hubbub on the streets of New York with their great towering skyscrapers made her feel bursting with energy, her faltering English was just enough to track down a dentist who could still Resi's pain. Then it was back to the hotel to dress up for an evening meal with Walter Wagner, a vice president of Paramount who had arranged to meet her with his wife.

He turned up alone, explaining that his wife was sick. Then they visited a club where liquor was poured secretively under the table, Prohibition was still in force, and the people acted as though it was a crime to sip a little alcohol. Before she knew what was happening, Wagner had her up on the floor dancing, pressing himself close, obviously expecting some gratitude from a new Paramount actress, who was to be paid the royal sum of over $1,000 a week. She let him chat away, hardly able to understand a word he said, he groped her in full view of everyone in the club as the alcohol did its work and the people quickly became thoroughly drunk. Marlene came from a tougher school where you had to learn how to carry on working even after you had been drinking half the night, the Americans could not take their drink and she began to see nightmare visions of a leering drunken face greedily trying to devour its fresh catch from old Europe. When Wagner took himself off to the gents, she fled back to her hotel, picked up the phone and rang Josef in Hollywood, explaining how she had given the slip to the vice president trying to get into her knickers. He listened attentively, asking exactly what had happened.

'Listen to me,' he said firmly, 'I want you to get packed and book the next train out to Chicago, leave tonight, before he comes looking for you, he's a big noise in the studio, you can't afford to upset him too much, it's the only way you'll get to avoid him.

'What now? Tonight?' she asked, feeling emotionally and physically exhausted after a helter skelter of activity all day long and then this drunken interruption to the evening.

'Go to Grand Central Station, now. Pack and go. I will meet you when you get near California, tell me what train you catch in Chicago. You understand.'

They spoke in German, he was her one lifeline in this altogether strange country. She agreed and told Resi to pack. In half an hour they were out the hotel and at the station, having told no one of their destination. Only when the train pulled out of Grand Central, in the middle of the night, could she relax. By late next morning they were in Chicago waiting for the train that would take them over the next two days to a new life in California. Slowly it dawned on her just how huge America was, even in Chicago after an all night journey they were still thousands of miles from their destination. After managing to phone von Sternberg in California she was told he would meet the train somewhere in New Mexico, she could not understand why they had to meet in a different country but did as she was told. All day long and all night they clattered over endless plains, the heat was intense in the private compartment, even with the blinds down. She surveyed the vast rolling fields, flat in every direction to the horizon, and realised how different and how empty this country was from her home in Europe where she was used to seeing villages and towns wherever she went, America seemed so underpopulated in comparison, and hot. The further south the train went, the hotter it got until she felt she was entering an inferno after her fateful decision to go to America, already she was sure she would never feel at home in the same way as in Germany, she was destined to wander the world, a gypsy nomad. Eventually she met Josef in New Mexico, only then realising they were still in America and not some part of Mexico. It took another day for them to reach California and von Sternberg had already arranged she attend a Hollywood social occasion that evening where the studio boss's daughter from the big rival studio of MGM, to which Greta Garbo was contracted, was holding a wedding party. She knew she was on display, being judged on her ability to rival their biggest star. She strode into the huge ballroom and reduced the mindless chatter of the assembled film crowd to silence as she followed behind von Sternberg who insisted on walking slowly from one end of the room to the other with her in tow. Finally, they all applauded her entrance and she could relax, her first show had gone well, just as she had planned. It was a bravura performance for someone who had spent all afternoon repairing the havoc that three days in a train had caused to their 'film star' looks. The whole of Hollywood was a film set, she realised, it was a company town, there was nowhere to go to relax, but she was determined to conquer it, just as surely as she had conquered Berlin after years of superhuman effort.

Josef von Sternberg was ready to shield her from the press and studio, he was not a man to relax his hold over her. On the set his word was law, and off it too he liked to organise and issue directives. The arrival in California had been carefully arranged so that the new star could be photographed by the press before being swept off in a limousine to prepare for her evening encounter. In the short time before they started filming at the beginning of June, he set about installing her in a suitable setting for a new Hollywood star, one who could rival Garbo in her allure and box office attraction. This lodestar to Marlene's imagination, the poor Swedish waif who had been transformed by her Svengali, Mauritz Stiller, into a creature of man and woman's desire, was not present at the MGM gathering. Marlene quickly learnt she protected her privacy with a passion, and she immediately decided to act in the same haughty way. At first, she was escorted by von Sternberg to the smarter restaurants like the Coconut Grove, and the Hollywood Roosevelt. More appealing to her was the Frisky Pom Pom Club with its chorus girl line-up of high kickers, that was the one place she felt at home in Hollywood, little did the audience realise that less than a year before she was still part of one of these chorus lines herself, German film wages bore no comparison to Hollywood's, $1,000 a week (worth more like $25,000 in purchasing power today) took getting used to. Von Sternberg strong-armed the studio into providing her with an apartment at Horn Avenue, just off Beverley Hills, that was furnished in film star kitsch, a multitude of mirrors and leopard skin furniture, all in the lastest Hollywood pastel colour style. The American film people had money but very little taste. Everything had to advertise its cost, there was never a hint of subtlety in all the vulgarity. The same was true about the Rolls Royce convertible allocated to her with her own chauffeur (she could not drive, and never wished to) but it did have the advantage for von Sternberg of being able to always keep track of his protégé's movements.

The West Coast women were enthusiastic practitioners of the healthy outdoor life, and used any excuse to shed most of their clothes. This lifestyle placed an emphasis on having a slim athletic body, whereas Marlene had a fuller more luscious figure. Her height of five foot five meant that tall elegance was not the immediate impression she gave. Von Sternberg insisted she come down to 9 stone from her more usual 10. Her first month was spent starving herself, alternated with visits to the Pacific seashore to walk along the white sands and experience a rare feeling of freedom in the already claustrophobic atmosphere of Hollywood. But work took first priority and from her arrival the studio backroom people were working on costumes and settings for the first American movie featuring the German star.

Before von Sternberg had left Europe for America, Marlene had suggested to him that he make a film of the book Amy Joly, which she put in his luggage when he sailed. Von Sternberg's boss, Schulberg, had been in Berlin to approve the US film contract, which was beyond von Sternberg's power to approve alone, the money men in the studio kept a tight hold on the finances. By the time she arrived in America, there was already a script written and the title had changed to Morocco after the leading male, Gary Cooper, had insisted that it was clear this was not simply a vehicle for the German Garbo.

Von Sternberg was adamant she lose all trace of her German accent for the American audiences, she was to be a mystery woman with an unknown past. In this, as in everything else, she went along with von Sternberg's creation of a femme fatale figure to rival the Swedish screen goddess, it was how he had sold her to the studio, and it was what had brought him to Europe when the Berlin film magazine had put Marlene and Garbo on their front cover at the beginning of 1928. Her 'discovery' by von Sternberg had been well signposted.

Soon they were filming the first scene, almost a recreation of her arrival in America, except that now her face was half hidden by a veil, she stared out from the deck's side at a new country, Morocco, while mist swirled around her. A smooth man with a neatly shaped moustache asked if he could help.

'I don't need any help,' Marlene replied dead pan, which took 40 takes to get exactly right as she struggled with the pronunciation of 'help'.

The smooth director with the neatly shaped moustache finally pronounced himself satisfied with the take and they prepared for the next day's shooting, in a Moroccan nightclub. Marlene added her own dash of daring to the filming, handing a rose to one of the women at a table after giving a performance in men's evening dress, then planting a kiss on her lips and leaving her with a suggestive look of merriment. For Marlene it was all good Berlin burlesque, in America it was going further than anyone else had done in suggesting that women could feel physical intimacy with each other. She realised any affairs with women in Hollywood needed to be handled with great discretion, even more than with the men. In the '20s, there had been a freewheeling attitude to censorship but by the time of Marlene's arrival Hollywood was trying to present a more apple pie image to its audiences in the American heartlands. The make-up of the film town was cosmopolitan, there were any number of Jewish film-makers who had decamped to the West Coast from the New York beginnings of film making in the previous 20 years. Like von Sternberg, they had escaped poverty in central Europe and the persecutions of the murderous Russian pogroms, but the new arrivals had quickly acquired the protective prejudices of a very rural West Coast, where the locals were cowboys who had pushed further and further west until they had found the sea. It was a rip roaring, get rich quick atmosphere, and all through the '20s great wealth had poured into the studios from a worldwide public with an insatiable desire for more and more entertainment. No hint of the Depression was allowed to filter onto the screen or even into the gilded film stars' lives. But the misery was there, the great void into which an actor could drop if they fell out of favour with the public just as suddenly as they had enjoyed its acclaim.

There was the sad story of Fatty Arbuckle, a comedian from the early '20s, who had experienced just such a meteoric rise and fall. There was talk of scandal, of how at a party they had all been drinking wildly when Fatty lured a girl into his room and cut her to pieces with a broken bottle inserted into her vagina, her screams went unanswered by the other guests, she had been rushed to hospital but died. He had tossed the bottle out the window saying 'there goes the evidence'. By the time of Marlene's arrival he was persona non grata in spite of escaping conviction at trial. Broke and alcoholic he was soon to die.

Marlene was experiencing the peculiar allure of star appeal for herself. Next door to her dressing room on the film lot was a young charming Frenchman, Maurice Chevalier, who quickly took her under his wing as another European far from home. Soon they were lovers and admirers, while von Sternberg could only fret at her inability to control her love desires, which appeared suddenly, capriciously and all-powerfully. Fame attracted Marlene as sure as any fan, as it had done from the times when she waited outside Berlin's studios for a glimpse of the female stars. But her more pressing concern was winning over her male lead, Gary Cooper. He was tall, stunningly handsome, all American, very direct and to the point, with no attempt at social graces. This disdain for European pretension could easily have shown itself on the film if she had not acted quickly. Cooper the film star and legionnaire enjoyed a night of passion with Marlene only to leave for the next battle. Marlene as Amy Jolly falls into the arms of the rich sophisticated artist who had befriended her on the boat. In the film she chose the safety and comfort of the rich artist. In life, she risked von Sternberg's wrath by bedding the American and giving him such fierce loving that his looks of gratitude on film needed no acting ability at all, it was for real. The film closes with her following his band of warriors out into the desert, casting away her sophisticated high heel shoes as she runs off into the setting sun in pursuit of true love, joining the women camp followers prepared to sacrifice all for their man. It remains a striking moment in her film history. In reality she chose von Sternberg and her career, the romance between her and Gary Cooper ended as the filming was completed. They stayed good friends, as Marlene sought to do with all her lovers.

There was no let-up in the frantic pace. Von Sternberg had already written a new film for her, called originally X-27. He had cast her as a Mata Hari spy, a street woman who understands the foibles and weaknesses of men, the streetwalker who wants to serve her country. It was another aspect of herself. As was the cool calculated treachery she had to employ on her victim: a Russian general who realises she has penetrated his disguise, and goes into a room to shoot himself before he has had the chance to enjoy her favours.

The firing squad awaits her in the film. But the streetwise X-27 coolly makes herself up for her next part, living out her claim to be not afraid of life, or of death. She insisted von Sternberg show her how she should fall when shot, every detail had to be right, and since she had never had a bullet slug enter her body, it had to be a carefully created effect. All Marlene's acting carried the stamp of every detail having been thought out and then faithfully enacted.

'Do I fall forwards or backwards when shot?' she demanded.

'Think of someone landing a terribly hard punch in your stomach,' von Sternberg volunteered.

Marlene crumpled up and fell sideways taking care to expose the famous limbs of 'Legs Dietrich' from Berlin's café society. The film recorded von Sternberg's discovery of her free, independent and treacherous nature. Yet even the treachery was balanced by a need to serve something higher, one's country, a cause. He discovered depths to her character which he then incorporated on film. And found these out the hard way, from their still changing relationship. They lived together more or less openly, though maintaining the pretence of two separate residences, but she still found herself drawn into other dalliances and it was a provocation von Sternberg could hardly accept.

However, their creative collaboration was bearing fruit. Morocco was previewed at a small town in California so that the film studio people could gauge the public's reaction. Marlene almost despaired when half of them left before the film had finished showing. She went home to pack, rang von Sternberg and announced she was returning to her husband and daughter.

'At least wait till we have shown the film,' he asked.

Unknown to her the critics had been favourably impressed at the preview, one even predicting that a great new star had been born. The film premiered at the end of November, followed a week later by the first American showing of The Blue Angel. The English film version of this was so difficult for the Americans to understand that the German subtitled version became more popular. But the Dietrich legs and garter caught the imagination of the great American public just as Emil Jannings had both feared and predicted. A new contract doubled her salary to $2,500 a week. She set sail for the London premiere, riding the waves of success. Again Morocco with its beautifully photographed sets and German expressionist atmosphere caught the public imagination. In time for Christmas she was back home in Berlin loaded down with gifts for Maria and Rudi, a star on both sides of the Atlantic. She wanted them to join her in Hollywood, the whiff of scandal was the only thing that could ruin her career, and what better cover could a young woman in Hollywood have than a devoted family with a beautiful 5 year old daughter? She shopped for the very best haute couture fashion, sending the bills onto von Sternberg. She was a moneymaker in the midst of an appalling economic slump and made the most of her good fortune, she had seen and experienced too much poverty to ever want to be dragged down to that level again, what was with you today would not necessarily be there tomorrow, all the trappings of fame and fortune could disappear in the murk of disaster on a worldwide scale. That seemed to be the situation as the American slump crossed over to Europe and Marlene saw the familiar hungry faces on Berlin's streets once again. It was Joyless Street, she could - but for her wits - be once again a wan, pinched face in the butcher's queque.

On her return to Berlin, Marlene quickly got in touch with her old friend, the singer Peter Kreuder. They worked on a song, Peter, which she recorded, and went out on the town to the theatres and shows, sat in the cafés, it was quite like old times except that the atmosphere was even more chaotic than she remembered on Berlin's streets. The economy seemed to be collapsing rapidly just as it had done in America a year earlier. Marlene knew she had to go back to America, it was a sweet interlude. This time she was determined to take back Maria with her. Rudi resisted at first, but he had her cheques and his woman Tamara to comfort him, Marlene realised how faraway she had grown from Maria, it was time to show her the sights and sounds of America.

Morocco was proving a fabulous success. Her acting, Lee Garmes' photography and von Sternberg's direction were all nominated for Academy Awards, although none were actually gained by their first American movie collaboration.

On return to America at the end of April, Marlene was stunned to be presented with a writ on the dockside by lawyers acting for Riza Royce von Sternberg, the scandal they had feared was in full public view as she accused Marlene of stealing her husband's affection. He had divorced her in June the previous year, shortly after Marlene's arrival in America, now Riza sought revenge.

Marlene pointed out her glamorous happy family, since Maria was living with her in Hollywood, and let the studio lawyers

85

persuade Riza to drop her lawsuit, which she did in return for a handsome payoff. American women were, Marlene realised, fascinated by money and power to a degree not known in Europe. It was a game whose rules she knew very well from Berlin. But this new element of scandal was something she had to handle very carefully indeed, the old freewheeling ways would have to be modified if she were to continue receiving her monthly cheques and the life it bought.

Chapter Eight

Shanghai Express

Marlene Dietrich felt relieved to be back in Hollywood after the tumult on the streets of Berlin and the shock of lawyers meeting her at the dockside in New York. Von Sternberg came up with a brilliant solution to the threatening scandal. He arranged for her to be photographed with Maria by the publicity people from the studio as they arrived back in California, there was a lot of resistance, but he got his way. Marlene suggested bringing over Rudi as well, with his Russian mistress kept discreetly in the background. Rudi agreed, after taking the bait of a job working for Paramount in Paris when he had performed his dutiful husband role in California. It took some time to win him over, he considered it a bad influence on Maria for von Sternberg to be staying in the same house as his wife and child. Marlene moved to a large house with a garden in North Roxbury Drive near Beverley Hills. It was a splendid house even by Hollywood's excessive standards of luxury. There were enough bedrooms for each person to sleep in a separate room and make their night-time assignations without disturbing the other occupants. It was all an elaborate game so that Maria did not know her mother was sleeping with a man who was not her husband. Rudi exempted his own arrangement with Tamara from this censoriousness and only agreed to let Maria stay in California - as Marlene's ultimate insurance against scandal - on condition that von Sternberg did not live so openly with his film protege,. After a month, when he was photographed everywhere in the company of Marlene, von Sternberg and Maria, Rudi departed in late August for Paris and his new job, the ever patient Tamara in tow.

Marlene immersed herself in preparations for her next film Shanghai Express and had staff to take care of Maria's needs for much of the day. There was Resi who acted as maid, while she had also brought over Gerda Huba, her old friend from when she first shared a flat in Berlin. Gerda became her personal assistant and adviser, helping with publicity and generally looking after Marlene's interests. It gave her some valuable company and support in what was still a very strange country. But the interludes when Maria and she went exploring the beaches of California, visiting the fun fairs and the broadwalk amusements, were becoming fewer and fewer as the time for filming got closer. By the autumn Josef von Sternberg was ready, he had worked with Jules Furthman on the script, an adaptation of a story by Harry Hervey, and was furiously recreating scenes from China on the studio lot, there was no expense spared on what was to become one of their most successful collaborations.

Shanghai Express is set on a train moving through a China where rival warlords have the country by the throat. To achieve these scenes in the studio, von Sternberg had a complete set built with a train, shanty town buildings, Chinese coolies, in fact all the hubbub of Peking Railroad Terminal and its approaches. His shot of the steaming train moving out through the bedlam of peasants and running chickens to its destination in Shanghai, is a masterpiece of the visual deception the best cinema can establish. Marlene worked long and hard with the costume designer Travis Banton to create just the right image for Shanghai Lily, a woman of mystery, well known as an adventuress and described as 'the white flower of the Chinese coast'.

While most of the action takes place on the train and at a station some hour away from Peking when the train is stopped by revolutionaries, it gave von Sternberg the opportunity to weave the magic of his favourite light and shade motif. He was still heavily influenced by the achievements of German Expressionist cinema, which was all but unknown in

Hollywood where there was little artistic aspiration, the box office was all.

The female lead wore black, an extremely difficult colour for the film stock to capture. Her close fitting black hat with exotic feathers, the veil, the pale contrasting white skin, all combined to produce a truly exotic woman, who had a mysterious past, von Sternberg's constant refrain in nearly all his work with Dietrich. Her character is established very early on, again one of his trademarks. A medical officer, the very British Clive Brook, of sleek good looks, encounters her on the train. He recognises her as an old flame, Madeline, but she tells him she has a new name. He asks if she is married, she slowly turns and says in that impassive voice von Sternberg loved so much, 'It took more than one man to change my name to Shanghai Lily.'

The old love is destined to reveal itself in an unusual way. The rebels threaten to put out the eyes of the British captain, Shanghai Lily decides to take up the rebel leader Chang's offer of becoming his mistress if he will spare the captain. The British officer, not realising what she is bartering, believes she has gone over to the other side. He is released and she is left behind. The rebel leader is killed by a woman who has been lying in wait for him, and Shanghai Lily rejoins the train in a scene where mayhem breaks out. The film closes with Shanghai Lily and Captain Hervey rediscovering their old love.

Three Academy nominations, for best picture, director and cameraman resulted in Lee Garmes picking up his justly deserved Academy Award for the film's cinematography. The film was a box office sensation that most bitter year of the Depression. The unemployed were everywhere, 25% of the population were out of work, despair lurked on the streets and people sought refuge in fantasy. Von Sternberg had created a suitable idol for them with his star's strangely immobile and distant face, it was an impassive mirror upon which the audience could project their own dreams. The cheeky mischievous witty Marlene of the Berlin night spots was replaced by a woman with a murky shadowy past and reputation, but still capable of gallant acts on behalf of a man she loved. A certain world weariness made the character more believable and intriguing, she represented loss of innocence, just as the real world realised the old simplicities were gone forever, if they had ever existed.

Paramount, never slow to realise the value of publicity, had poured $500,000 into the virtual double release of Morocco and The Blue Angel at the end of the previous year, but as Shanghai Express reached the nation's picture palaces they pulled out all the stops and Marlene's star shone as never before. This box office popularity was not an asset to be wasted.

Von Sternberg demanded total control for the next picture, to be called Blonde Venus. And this demand was to cause serious strife between him and the studio production chief Schulberg. It boiled up over a scene where Marlene was to play a mother reduced to prostitution in order to provide for her young son. Typically, von Sternberg wanted the child to be present but hidden under a bar table as the negotiation with Cary Grant for her favours was conducted. With increasing pressure from the League of Decency and other custodians of the public morals, Hollywood was having to tone down its pictures in order not to threaten the social order. What the film had to do with people's moral behaviour is more questionable, families were being broken apart all over the country because of the still worsening Depression.

Von Sternberg wanted to end his association with Marlene Dietrich after Shanghai Express, it had gone as far it could go he judged, and the artist in him wanted to move on. The love affair had cooled to a close working relationship where Marlene depended on von Sternberg to guide her, and bring out whatever aspect of her character he had divined necessary for the part. But there were other attractions for her highly active libido in the glamorous film world. She met a glorious Spanish dancer, Imperio Argentina, in one of the clubs and fell in love with her, inviting her back to her house so that she could cook and fuss over her, a trait which inevitably came to the fore when Marlene fell for one of her own sex. But this infatuation was too much for Imperio's husband who arrived one night with boat tickets to Mexico for the dancer and himself. The Spanish beauty's departure left a great blank in Marlene's life, Hollywood breathed a sigh of relief. Even though she had taken to largely wearing trousers and a man's jacket when seen about town, the film crowd refused to see any more in this than eccentricity, rather than a display of masculine bravura designed to dazzle potential female admirers, which is what it really was. For many American women in Hollywood, this cross-dressing by the exotic German star was a great come-on.

But as filming was getting underway finally, tragedy not scandal struck. The Lindbergh baby was kidnapped and killed. Shortly afterwards Marlene received a letter formed out of newspaper headings. It demanded $10,000 to stop Maria being kidnapped. Von Sternberg proved a tower of strength. Bars were added to all their home's windows, armed guards stood in the garden when Maria went to swim in the pool, and the child accompanied her mother to the studio rather than staying at home with her governess. Every waking hour they were all on guard against any threat to Maria's life. Another German woman, the wife of a milliner, had received a similar kidnap note which demanded she leave some money by a tree. The potential kidnappers were amateurs, for they confused the note for Marlene with the one for the milliner's wife and then complained Marlene had only left a few dollars for them at the drop off point. She never heard from them again, but it ruined any thought of her going out all summer.

The opening of Blonde Venus proved a surprising success in the autumn. For the first time she was portrayed singing on film. In one number she emerged from a gorilla outfit in a blonde wig to perform her nightclub routine. She was back in the club world, another aspect of Marlene that von Sternberg incorporated into the script he put together after rejecting numerous Paramount offerings. The twist in the story was that she was performing to finance an operation for her husband who was dying because there was no money to pay for hospital treatment. Eventually she finds fame and success and returns to the family for the obligatory happy ending, but not before falling for the charms of Cary Grant on screen and off it. Although as he was a confirmed but secret homosexual, no sexual demands were involved in the very public pairing.

Even though the film took more then $3,000,000 at the box office, von Sternberg was insistent to his bosses that it was time for him to move on. They agreed, Marlene was given to director Rouben Mamoulian for a film called *Song of Songs*. Its most memorable demand involved Marlene posing nude for a sculpture of herself created by the young artist in the film who has fallen in love with his model. The sculpture was anatomically correct in all details, for Marlene gladly volunteered her services for the commissioning of the sculpture. In the film the audience sees little more in the flesh than the ankles of a simple serving girl in a bookshop, but the shots of the statue raised the sexual temperature of the film considerably, there was little doubt who had modelled for it. The film's other claim to fame is the song Jonny which Fredrich (now Frederick) Hollander had composed in 1920, and recorded in Germany in 1929. English lyrics were now added by Edward Heyman. The film also introduced Marlene to the British actor Brian Aherne who became a great friend both to her and to daughter Maria for the next few years. Some of the press, at least, waxed lyrically over the poetic treatment Mamoulian had achieved. It showed Marlene was capable of performing outside of Josef von Sternberg's direction, but the sexual allure Mamoulian saw was that of a simple country girl with a body appealing to older men - such as himself. There were no undertows of darker knowledge in this depiction of her attractions that von Sternberg might have achieved.

The film had turned out quite well, some critics thought it one of her better performances. Little did they realise how inwardly she had trembled at the thought of losing her guide and mentor as he inexplicably deserted her and suggested Mamoulian as director. When the New Year opened she had refused to appear on the set. Law suits threatening her entire earnings for years to come (a massive $189,000) were commenced. Her lawyer, Ralph Blum, came to the beach house she was renting in Santa Monica on Ocean Highway to interrupt her reverie while sharing the house with close friend and indefatigable charmer, Maurice Chevalier. Marlene toyed with the idea once again of returning to Germany. A fortuitous tip enabled her to engage the services of Garbo's agent, Harry Edington, who was to protect her for long afterwards from the Hollywood sharks. A salary of $4,500 a week was negotiated in a new contract that would run for five years. After a week she capitulated to the studio under these new terms. Even though the most famous actress in America, Marlene Dietrich found she had less power than the Paramount's studio moguls, Schulberg and his cohort Cohen. The negotiations were helped when Lubitsch, the head director at the studio, reported back that Dietrich and Garbo were the two most famous stars in Europe, especially important when overseas earnings represented nearly half of the Hollywood studios' incomes. Even though they had not met, Garbo's and Dietrich's lives continued to grow in parallel to one another. The Swedish star was to also share her lover when Mercedes de Costa, a Mexican lady of some 40 years, walked into Marlene's life.

Mercedes was small, dark, intense, a firefly of a woman. Her brain was as sharp and incisive as a man's, her soul was filled with poetry and beauty. She wrote screenplays for a living, but perhaps her greatest attraction was that she was - or had been - Greta Garbo's lover, and nothing acted so powerfully on Marlene's imagination as the opportunity to get close to her rival's lover - and so to Garbo herself. To steal Mercedes from Garbo, Marlene wooed the physically tiny Mexican lady with a demonic passion. Dozens and dozens of flowers were despatched to her door each day, Marlene asked for nothing more than to serve her, pamper her, prepare her little intimate meals while Mercedes regaled Marlene with her wild stories and even wilder style and presence. Poetry ran through her veins. Soon the Mexican was living with Marlene and Maria, and to please her Marlene wore her mannish outfits more and more often, caring little for the ensuing scandal. They formed a girl buddy group with her friends and went out on the town together, making sure they were seen in all the best cafés, it was quite like Berlin again. Voices whispered, but Maria's presence stilled the wagging tongues. Marlene's name was not linked to any men, and who was to say it was not all good girlish fun? It was not by any means so innocent but the Americans had little imagination in these matters, it was unthinkable to most.

After *Song of Songs* Marlene returned to Paris with Maria, Rudi booked them into the best hotels and they lived the life of royalty, visiting Rudi's parents in Austria and spending idyllic days on the Riviera. Here she could unwind, and make use of her fluent language ability to the full, they compensated them selves for the lack of culture in Hollywood by tasting the best of the old Europe. But with Hitler in charge in Germany, Marlene had a presentiment she should stay away from her homeland in spite of offers she received to return as the leading light of German cinema. Marlene was told by his representatives that Hitler admired her films, and later still she learnt that when the Nazis banned *The Blue Angel* as a slur on German womanhood, Hitler kept a copy of the film for himself which he played endlessly. However she had little illusion that the attraction lay in the region of her garter belt. There were even suggestions that Rudi should return as head of UFA to replace the Jews who had run it, and then fled. For as soon as Hitler seized power, the persecution of Jews in any position of power commenced, just as Hitler had laid down in his plan of action, '*Mein Kampf*', an exact description of the evil he planned to let loose on the world. The wise ones among the Jewish community left immediately, more than 200,000 followed during the next five years, but many stayed behind and Marlene learned later how some of them had died in the concentration camps. The Germany she knew was gone. Berlin actresses like Leni Riefenstahl, who had been a friend in her café society days, welcomed the German renaissance and their careers prospered as the Nazi engineered revival of the economy got underway with dizzying speed. Leni Riefensthal fell under his spell, and even arranged to meet him, though she stopped short at joining the Nazi party. But the Führer held no such spell for Marlene Dietrich. To her, he was a jumped-up corporal, no part of the great military tradition her father had embodied. The attractions of America and Hollywood seemed infinitely greater. The Germans next tried to discredit her, claiming she had sent a cheque to a Nazi film institute. Later the world learnt that her cheque for $500 had been sent to help the poor children in Schoenberg, the district in Berlin where she had grown up. As the lazy summer days on the Riviera drew to an end, Marlene returned refreshed to America, and another collaboration with von Sternberg. The studio had him in their grasp, just as much as Marlene , not least because of the alimony payments he was making to his ex-wife Riza Marks.

Chapter Nine

The Devil is a Woman

The parallels in the life of Garbo and Dietrich continued. The project that von Sternberg had in preparation was a life story of Catherine the Great of Russia. He was undoubtedly attracted to the subject by the proven stories of her insatiable sexual appetite. Meanwhile Garbo was also working on a film portraying Catherine the Great, and yet a third production was in hand with Elizabeth Bergner playing the lead role under the direction of Alexander Korda. It had to be more than a coincidence that the creative galaxy of talent in Hollywood all began to spin out tales of this legendary woman from exotic old Europe. Hollywood was a small town, people talked, the rivalry between the European stars was intense, they were the vehicles for the studio bosses' dreams of avarice.

But while Marlene concentrated on creating the right visual impact for Catherine as a Russian queen, von Sternberg was at work on every detail of the film. He was determined to make the most of the medium, using sound to overwhelm the cinemagoers' senses. Marlene's own contribution was to create a Catherine swathed in white fur from head to toe, and in one of her favourite scenes from the film, she rides a white stallion up a staircase at the head of her troops. The resonance of the horses' hoofs and this army of marching boots was captured in perfect reverberating tone by von Sternberg on the sound track.

Yet the story of the film was somehow lost among the vast sets, with 12-foot high gargoyles, threatening statues and sheer excess of ornamentation, it was a court run riot in sensual abandon that had descended to the depravities of sado-masochism in all its varieties. Her depiction of a shy German girl gradually turning into a woman of insatiable appetite for men was carefully orchestrated by von Sternberg. It hinted at a Europe where dark fantasies and madness lurked beneath the glittering facades. It was not difficult to see in the fate of the hapless Grand Duke Peter, the Queen's husband, a prediction of von Sternberg's own demise from top level movie-making. Madness plagued his character, the weird and the phantasmagorical take over, until there is only an inevitable dissolution into chaos.

The film failed miserably at the box office, all the more galling because Korda's far more realistic and straightforward *Catherine the Great* had done well in February. In spite of holding *The Scarlet Empress* - as it became - till late in the year von Sternberg lost all surprise for his exotic period piece. This failure, after a long string of success, persuaded von Sternberg that their artistic collaboration was undoubtedly near its end, but he was forced to stay for at least one more picture because of his precarious financial situation. He lived the part of the great director in his life off-set, it was not a way of life that came cheap.

The new film became *The Devil is a Woman*, a script suggested by Mamoulain, and is the closest depiction of how von Sternberg saw Marlene Dietrich. Marlene believed he caught her at her most beautiful playing Concha Perez, a bar dancer and singer, a woman who uses men for what she can get, with little or no regret. Her relationship with von Sternberg had assumed most of these characteristics. After the film's hero, Don Pasqaul (Lionel Atwill from *Song of Songs*), has lavished all his affection and money on her she disappears from his life, only for him to find her five years later in a Cadiz bar, with a young political refugee, Antonio Galvan (Cesar Romero) as her devoted admirer. The men fight a duel over her, Don Pasqaul deliberately loses the contest and is wounded, she visits him in hospital then heads for the border with the handsome young politician, only to turn back at the last minute for her previous lover, now hopeless and abandoned.

Set in Spain in the 1890s, it still managed to upset the Spanish authorities with its suggestion that the Spanish Civil Guard cared immensely for drinking and little or nothing for correct behaviour. Paramount withdrew the film from European release, but it had already been shown in America to unenthusiastic reviews and attendances. Most critics labelled the film slow and ponderous, though there was some admiration for the sets and the photography. Von Sternberg's considered slow rhythm in his films no longer caught the national mood which longed for excitement and realism. His work always contained undertones and nuances, he had never really lost his penchant for mood and ambience rather than plot and action. He told Marlene on the set even before the film was finished that their collaboration was over, she was unnerved and believed it was to do with the strain of filming. Von Sternberg was particularly brutal in his direction, reducing his star to tears. She, who had long learnt to obey his every wish no matter how many times he asked for a scene to be played again, till he had complete satisfaction. There was no pleasing him. They had finally used up all the goodwill their long partnership had established.

Marlene wondered how she would survive in the Hollywood film world without her protecting guide, yet she should not have worried, for it was he who had really come to the end of his career rather than herself. Although a few other films followed, von Sternberg was never again to enjoy the top billing that had been his during their long collaboration over seven films and five years. He was the perfect technician and had even been the camera lighting man on their last film, having at last gained his union membership. Even before this there was no detail too small for him to consider in a film's production.

Their most entrancing times together had been at the very beginning when she was the sorcerer's apprentice as he revealed to her his art night after night going through the rushes of *The Blue Angel*. She learned about film lighting and camera work watching him editing the film frame by frame with endless patience, the fragmented segments all falling into place thanks to his visual imagination. He created the film star legend that was Marlene, not least with his lighting that threw shadows under her high Teutonic cheek bones and gave her face the vacant glazed look onto which the Depression-crazed audiences could project their simmering sexual fantasies. He never left old Vienna mentally and artistically. While visiting the art galleries of North America in his destitute early years he took his greatest inspiration from his gifted countrymen, artists like Gustav Klimt. That late flowering of the Habsburg Empire produced its finest work just as the curtains were coming down on the centuries-long period of power and influence. In the New World, this exoticism had to be disguised in the stories of gangsters and love and romance, but the darker side is always there, told by a troubled soul who knew all there was to know of humiliation and depravity.

The woman he created gradually became Marlene Dietrich on screen and off. She learnt to position a full length mirror just to the side of the camera so that she could hold her head in the right way to catch the all-important light. It always had to come from high above to catch her face's bone structure in the right way. The Berlin nose operation had straightened her profile, and no lights were allowed to appear behind her face. It would have lit up her nose and produced a bulbous effect, hinting at peasant ancestry on her mother's side, rather than the perfection which she sought as a movie star. It was a very studied art, learnt from von Sternberg more than anybody. The essential attraction for him, as for everyone else, was her legs. In the audition for The Blue Angel she made sure they were displayed to full effect while seated upon the piano. The man was hooked, just as the cinema audiences were to be hooked. It helped that Paramount's enormous publicity campaign for Morocco and The Blue Angel when they opened back to back in America in late 1931 also concentrated on her legs, they created just as much sexual intrigue and excitement in America as they had in Berlin. Maria suffered from Marlene's all-consuming leg fixation. For two years in her childhood she decreed that she be in leg irons to straighten her legs. The likelihood is there was nothing wrong with them. Then on arrival in America, the child had to play the perfect blonde angel in support of Marlene's starring role as movie star. The highlight for her childhood came when she played the young Catherine the Great so sweetly that she earned high praise from the critics. But her mother expected nothing less.

Von Sternberg made another seven movies during the rest of his life, which came to an end in 1969. He attended movie buff festivals around the world, and was in some demand from film students who appreciated what he had achieved in the films he made with Marlene. But further fame eluded him . He was a despot on set, and the exact opposite in bed, demanding to be dominated just as much as he demanded to be the dominator in the public world. Marlene suffered his daytime demands without complaint and then extracted her own compensation in the night when he would plead for mercy from his dominatrix who instinctively saw his need for abject humiliation that was gladly delivered.

In Hollywood such propensities had to be kept very quiet. It was the moral equivalent of Kansas, this alleged capital of the movie world. Scandal could finish a career as the studio bosses lived in fear of their films and their stars being banned by the increasingly vocal and powerful League of Decency. Von Sternberg, after he separated from Marlene Dietrich, was caught up in a scandal which effectively finished Lionel Atwill's Hollywood career. Apart from playing Marlene's lover in *Song of Songs* and *The Devil is a Woman*, Atwill had created a screen persona which owed much to his appearing in a horror movie called Dr X as a mad bad doctor. After his divorce from his wife, who had been married to the future General Macarthur, he devoted his weekends to holding wild parties where all the guests joined in the sexual frolics. Von Sternberg was in attendance at one of these parties when scandal broke out over a 16-year-old girl who claimed she had been made pregnant at the party. Two court cases later, Atwill was convicted of perjury, though not of holding an orgy, the studio bosses would not touch him after that.

It was while breaking with von Sternberg that scandal came closest to Marlene Dietrich. She had been introduced to John Gilbert by Mercedes de Costa. He had also been Garbo's lover both on and off screen. The actor had a heavy drink problem but gradually as their romance and friendship blossomed she was weaning him off the drink and instilling in him a love of good food, moonlight drives and swimming pool exercise. But there were demons eating away at his soul, not the least that his career was fading and he would still seek the answer in alcoholic forgetfulness. He was the great lover of the silent screen and had propelled Garbo to fame as he played the English Valentino to her Scandinavian ice maiden. The arrival of the talkies meant that a different kind of actor was required, and although Garbo manoeuvred for him to be her co-star in *Queen Christina*, his glory days were over. At 36, because of his perpetual drinking, he looked much older. But the allure he had on screen, smouldering sensuality behind his sleek English good looks, he also possessed in person. Marlene was besotted with him. He was divorced and had a child of 10 when they began their affair. It was another link in their shared fortunes, for although her theoretical marriage protected Marlene from the studio bosses' dictates on what was acceptable behaviour, she had to be careful to maintain her cover. She insisted that she visit Gilbert at his house for a night of love, rather than have him stay with her and Maria. The affair was intense, passionate, everything a woman could ask for from a man. He was also considerate and tactful. At one point she was pregnant with his child, but as he was not ready for marriage she decided to terminate the pregnancy. The ardour between them continued.

With von Sternberg no longer her director, she realised she would have to take a far more active role in the production of her films. The project that the studio suggested was eventually called Desire after the first title of *The Pearl Necklace* was dropped. Ernst Lubitsch was running Paramount as the head of production, since Shulberg had gone over to Universal taking von Sternberg with him. Marlene fought hard for John Gilbert to be given the male lead in this modern light comedy.

The film revolved around a story of a professional French jewel thief, Madeleine de Beaupre, smuggling out a pearl necklace in the jacket of American tourist Tom Bradley (played by her old lover Gary Cooper) when she reaches Spanish customs after swindling a French jeweller out of the necklace. Needless to say a comedy of errors follows, with Marlene trying to drive off in Gary Cooper's car after they have successfully crossed the border, only to find that the necklace is still in his possession. He discovers the plot and realises he's been duped, that the woman's love is counterfeit. It is actually for real, as he finally realises and all ends happily with Tom and Madeleine heading for love and marriage in Detriot. The film proved a great success with both audiences and critcs, Frank Nugent in the New York Times writing that Marlene had recaptured some of the freshness and gaiety of her Blue Angel days now that she was freed from acting the passive female of von Sternberg's fevered imagination. She was allowed to show real feelings for Gary Cooper, then at the height of his all-American attractiveness for cinema audiences. But the sunny faced Madeleine was actually hiding a lot of pain. Tragedy had struck two days before shooting for the film began.

John Gilbert had already suffered two minor heart attacks during the period of their romance, and as the New Year opened they met up again at his home for a night of passion. Hardly had they begun making love when he was shaken by a terrible pain in his chest.

She heard the gurgling noise in his throat as he collapsed on top of her while still making love. The gasping mouth of John was right next to her ear, she froze as the gasps turned to groans of extreme pain. Summoning up her full strength she prised his prostrate form out of her and threw him over on his side in an instinctive way, aware that he must be breathing his last.

'What is it?' she demanded in a quiet urgent voice of alarm.

'My chest, my chest,' he groaned, as he lay beside her awkwardly frozen by the pain. Marlene sat above him pushing vigorously down on his chest to keep him breathing, but it seemed to make no difference, he subsided into gentle moaning, hardly moving as the heart attack convulsed his body again.

'My darling, you need help,' she whispered, realising that she could not afford to be found in bed with Gilbert when he gave every indication of dying.

Her mind raced. A doctor had to come to him just as soon as she could leave the house and remove all signs of her visit. She rang home for her chauffeur, telling him to come immediately. By the time he arrived she was dressed and packed, having checked round the house to make sure it looked like John Gilbert had spent the night at home by himself. She asked the chauffeur to call her doctor as she left, leaving the door on the latch. There was no sound coming from John Gilbert, he simply lay where the heart attack had seized him, but now he was dressed in his pyjamas. Distraught as she was, she knew she had to get out of there as fast as possible. Only after she had left was the doctor allowed to come to John Gilbert's house. He died just as they got him to hospital, and it was recorded he died alone. The wild drinking had taken its toll and he knew only too well that his star was no longer in the ascendant. It was a setback for Marlene, a time of depression, but she could not show all her grief. Her soldier father's training meant that she carried on her life as though nothing too much had happened. There was only one rule in Hollywood, that was survival. All around she watched the stars come and go driven by the insufferable swings of capricious fate. She did what she could for his widow and daughter, but John Gilbert left his family remarkably little. There was a sad auction of his effects. Marlene bid for most of them, especially his bed sheets, paying a vastly inflated price. She became an unofficial godmother to his daughter for years afterwards.

To help explain these sudden falls from grace, Marlene started to develop an interest in astrology. It was to be a source of comfort for the rest of her life. Friends were sent their horoscopes by her Californian astrologer, Carroll Richter, no big decisions were made until she had had a reading to establish the propitiousness of the time. Most reassuring of all for her was to be told that she had been born to be a movie star. On the cusp of the fifth house of entertainment in perfect alignment, was Neptune, the planet of moviemaking. It was ordained that she should be in films, and that was comforting to know. Nevertheless she had to work day and night at perfecting her craft, it did not come easily, every line and every look had to be rehearsed and then repeated until it was perfect. Then she could hold that look, that stance, for long periods of time without moving at all until it was in the can. That is the true demand of the movies, an infinite patience to get things exactly right.

During the affair with John Gilbert, Marlene met Garbo for the first time. It was arranged through Mercedes de Costa who persuaded the Swedish superstar to come to a party at Marlene's insistence. When Marlene got close to Greta Garbo's face she saw that the Swede's eyelashes had been braided together to make them stand out. She realised the time and patience involved in such an arrangement, it would take four or five hours to achieve this perfection of the make-up artist's craft. But she had learned from both Mercedes and John Gilbert that the woman was a true professional, married to her art. In this they were sisters, even if they had never previously met in the incessant whirl of Hollywood parties and dinners. Marlene, like Garbo, preferred long leisurely drives in the country, walking and hiking in the open country around Hollywood or down by the sea, rather than the closed small world of the parties and dinners where the same select circle of people circulated.

Garbo's former lovers, and in John Gilbert's case still occasional existing lover, gave Marlene fresh insights into her appeal. Her poor background, with a father who died early, just like Marlene's father, were part of the answer. Marlene heard about her life in Stockholm at the turn of the century where she had to struggle through ice and snow each day of the terrible winters. One day, acting on some kind of presentiment, Greta Gustafson had gone out to look for her father, whom she found lying stretched out in a fierce snow storm freezing to death. In spite of her efforts, he had died. She found work in a cheap hairdressers, while she hovered around the theatre world. Her discovery by a Svengali- like Jewish mentor followed. Mauritz Stiller had come to California with her and then been manoeuvred out of control of her professional life by the studio bosses. Garbo was a peasant, with a peasant's instincts for survival. Marlene's days in Berlin had taught her a similar streetwise appreciation of the essential facts of life. But apart from this one meeting their paths had never crossed, Garbo remained very much the star of MGM studios and Dietrich of Paramount. They were employees of competing studios, and hence deadly rivals in that company town which Marlene endeavoured to leave each year for a long vacation in Europe where gracious living and sanity prevailed.

Chapter Ten

The highest-paid woman in the world

Marlene's desire to escape to Europe and away from her sadness after the loss of John Gilbert could not be put into effect when filming commenced on what became called I Loved a Soldier. It was a remake of the 1927 silent movie Hotel Imperial in which the beautiful dark-eyed Pola Negri had starred. With von Sternberg she had always faithfully followed his direction. But working under a new director, Henry Hathaway, and with a script about which she had her doubts, she took every advantage of the contract which stated she had final say over the script. Within four days she had fallen out with the producer, Benjamin Glazer, to such an extent that he refused to continue working with her, stating as his reason that he was not going to allow a star to have so much authority over a story he was supervising.

Marlene's old friend, Ernst Lubitsch, head of production, took over the film while the script was rewritten by Grover Jones and Henry Hathaway. But the problems continued. Ernst Lubitsch suddenly announced he was going to Europe for three months, having fallen out with his bosses and William Le Baron became head of production as well as taking over the film. With him Marlene found no rapport at all, at the end of a tortuous month she consulted her agent who found a let-out for her in the contract: no Lubitsch, no Dietrich. She walked out, with the costs of production already $900,000.

The studio tried to save the situation by bringing in another actress, Margaret Sullavan. But the film was jinxed. The new female lead fell over some cables while being pursued by one of her co-stars, Stuart Erwin, and broke two bones in her arm. Marlene's male lead had been Charles Boyer, newly arrived from France, and she had seen enough of his abilities to mentally tick him off for her next film vehicle. It was not until 1939 that Hotel Imperial was finally shot and released by Paramount, this time with Isa Miranda in Marlene's role, she even looked like her.

At the time the whole situation seemed unbearable, but there was an unexpected lucky break for her as rumours circulated about John Gilbert's death and her part in it. She did indeed blame herself for what had happened and kept a votive candle burning at home in front of his picture. Her private grief had intruded into her professional work, she realised this, and was only too glad when David Selznick contacted her for one of the earliest colour films using extra lifelike 3-colour Technicolor. Paramount, not having a vehicle for their star, were obliged to pay her $250,000 and happily acceded to Selznick's request to loan Dietrich out for his company's production which was to be released through United Artists. A splendid fee of $200,000 was negotiated through her agent, Harry Eddington, and she set about finding the right costume for a film that was to be made largely in the desert.

It was back to the themes of Morocco: desert, doomed love, endless vistas, spiritual crisis. The story revolved around Marlene being told to go to the desert by Mother Josephine, her convent headmistress and confidante. There, the nun says, she will find peace. She was looking for comfort after spending years nursing her dying father. On the train journey to the Algerian desert she meets a brooding Charles Boyer who, though she does not know it, is a former Trappist monk determined to see life outside his monastery. On the train journey this strange handsome man is rude to her, but they meet up again in the town of Benimora where two Algerians have taken her to a nightclub to see some dancers perform. A riot ensues as the fiery dancers, who include Tilly Losch, provide the evening entertainment and Marlene is rescued by Charles Boyer. A fated friendship develops. A sand diviner predicts the couple will take a trip and enjoy great happiness, he then abruptly halts his predictions. The couple marry and head off for a desert honeymoon.

At the desert encampment, a group of French soldiers stumble upon them and one of the soldiers recognises Charles Boyer. Gradually the soldier works out where he has seen him before. Marlene discovers from him that her husband is a runaway monk and after 20 minutes agonising on screen she urges him to return to his monastery, with her making her tearful farewell at the gates. Fade.

The gossip around town was that Garbo had been offered the part but recognised the ending for what it was - pure kitsch. She, with her down to earth instincts, knew that no girl would deliver her lover back into the arms of the church, sins of the flesh had no worry for her and for most of the cinema audiences. But Selznick had challenged Marlene about her reputation for being difficult, she was told to not interfere in the script as the price of the job. But post-von Sternberg, she found myself wanting to take charge of all the details of production as they affected her. She knew how her hair should be, and insisted that her devoted friend and hairdresser, Nellie Manley, reset the dampened flat tresses between takes. The heat was unbearable in the Mohave desert, it reached 138 degrees, and lifeless limpid hair was just one of the penalties of the furnace the crew and cast worked in.

Marlene's mobile caravan became a refuge to which she returned whenever possible even trying to get Joshua Logan, the assistant director, on her side in a half-baked plot to replace Richard Bolesawaski, the director, with von Sternberg. But nothing came of it, though von Sternberg was keen. Selznick, equally obsessive in his own way, was demanding that Bolesawaski act as dictatorially as von Sternberg on set and control Marlene. But she got her way on colour, wearing a white dress set off with vivid touches of brilliance in the scarf. While her hair, actually a reddish dark blonde colour, was dyed to a more Swedish blonde for the benefit of the expensive film stock.

This part of her performance did succeed. The film won an Academy Award for W Howard Greene's cinemaphotography while Time magazine in an article later that year wrote:

'If The Garden of Allah's weak point is its story, its strong point is its female star. In the first place, to Marlene Dietrich's golden hair and porcelain skin, color is more complimentary than it has been to any other actress who has so far tried it. In the second place, the North African desert is her speciality. In the third place, if there is any actress in Hollywood who cinema addicts have always yearned to see in the flesh - to which color film is the closest practical approach - Marlene Dietrich is the one.'

She had worked hard for that quote and the front cover on Time magazine. Their reporter had been in London when later in the year she was working on Knight Without Armour for Alexander Korda, who she had first worked with in Berlin. The reporter was there for a shot where she takes a bubble bath. Ignoring the convention of appearing in a skin coloured swimsuit Marlene peeled off and arrived on set naked to step into the bubbles. Somehow she fell on the slippery surface and ended up legs akimbo facing the assembled film crew and reporter. With a laugh and a winning smile in his direction, she picked herself up and plopped down among the bubbles. He was smitten.

It was while she was in London for the filming that Marlene had another approach from the Nazis. The first had been in Paris the previous year. It was necessary for her to renew her passport and, accompanied by Rudi, she went to the German embassy. Rudi wanted to go inside with her but she pointed out the danger.

'Step inside this door, and you are on German territory. They won't dare detain me, but you are a different matter.'

'You think I am afraid?' Rudi asked.

'You ought to be. Just wait here, I will be as formal and as proper as the occasion demands, they won't dare try anything.'

Marlene less sure of this fact than she sounded. Rudi and Marlene had arranged to meet her mother and sister just over the border in Austria that summer, rather than return to Berlin. Her mother and sister could not see what was happening, indeed her sister was married to a man who was a strong Nazi sympathiser, and Marlene had doubts about her sister too, she was all too German in her willingness to bend down before a powerful figure.

Marlene was escorted along a long corridor and ushered into a huge room decorated with a great Nazi flag behind a chair where the ambassador himself sat. On either side stood two six foot German soldiers from the SS. But the ambassador was charm itself.

'Miss Dietrich, it is an honour to meet such an internationally famous German actress.'

She sat down gracefully and obliged with a half smile, no more. The ambassador continued.

'You wish to renew your German passport?'

She nodded.

'There is no problem, certainly we will be honoured to give you a renewal. You are not planning to return to Germany at the moment?'

The two guards stood rigidly at attention as he spoke. She was only too aware that if she said the wrong thing, the situation could change in a flash, there was a massive sureness and arrogance about these two guards, a token of the rapidly growing armed forces who backed the ambassador's words.

He leant forward almost imperceptibly on his walnut desk which was as huge as the room.

'I have been authorised to make an offer to you, which will assist your film career, by the very highest authorities in Germany,' he said quietly, studying her face.

'Please tell me more,' she demurely replied, knowing what was coming.

'The German film industry is expanding its production of films as I am sure you know. If you were to return to Germany we could guarantee lead parts of your own choosing and budget would be no problem.'

'I would have to have choice of director,' she said, knowing that von Sternberg would not be welcome in the exclusively German film industry.

'Yes, of course, who did you have in mind?'

'Josef von Sternberg.'

'But, Miss Dietrich, he is a Jew. We are talking about German culture and German cinema, you would be working with your own kind.'

Marlene got up to go.

'There must be a way to arrange such a thing,' she stated.

The ambassador rose.

'I have arranged for your passport to be renewed. You can collect it from the reception desk on the way out. I will pass on your request to Berlin.'

The guards accompanied her down the long corridor to the reception desk where she was handed her renewed passport. They turned round at the door of the embassy and Marlene fell into Rudi's arms, trembling after the eerily threatening interview and the side effects of the pills she had swallowed so hastily

'Rudi, Rudi, you must never go back to Germany while that madman is in control. These people will stop at nothing, I know that, I felt it in there,' she gasped to the very supportive and understanding Rudi.

But the man who it was rumoured had played The Blue Angel over and over to himself did not give up so easily. In London, he had a more subtle agent, the wife of Marlene's former Berlin agent Mady Soyka, to make her an even more compelling offer. The conversation took place in her dressing room during filming of Knight without Armour.

Mady, who was an actress in her own right, played on their previous friendship. She had a journalist with her, but it was all kisses and sighs between the two women. Then she pulled Marlene into a corner and whispered.

'I have a fantastic offer for you, Marlene. Josef Goebbels wants you to do a film in Germany, just for a month, and you will be paid in British pounds, 50,000 pounds, tax free. What do you say?'

'I am very surprised,' she said looking her up and down, surprised how even Mady was hand in glove with the Nazis.

'But I am under contract for the next two years. Perhaps we should talk in 1940 or 1941 after my commitments are taken care of.'

Mady returned her icy stare and suddenly walked away, the Nazis and their followers were so used to getting what they wanted by intimidation that they did not know what to do when someone stood up to them, a lesson western Europe was very slow to learn. After that Marlene had one more overture from Berlin. It increased her sense of urgency to get American citizenship, realising that she no longer had a home in her own country and America, despite all its alien qualities, offered the only safe haven in the coming storm. She left Hitler to his own sordid imaginings, but it is doubtful if his sex drive was his guiding force, there had been whispers that he was a very uninspiring lover, while others spoke of his wish to degrade women, as he had with his niece. He was also said to like to be abused by his women, and preferred the simple working class girl Eva Braun to the sophisticated women he felt obliged to be seen with in public. The man was seedy, insipid even, until he had an audience which he could use to suck in their energy. He was empty, a vampire who stole energy and life from those who possessed it, he himself was almost a disincarnate ghoul, and all the more evil because of it. Marlene never underestimated him or the damage he could cause, there were many men like this to be found in the shadowy world of the nightclubs, the ghouls who come out by night is how she thought of them. Life in the flesh had little appeal, it was power they sought, to remedy their own inadequacies. Their outward sadism was balanced by an inner need for punishment in their private lives such as they were.

Other German actresses were not so immune to the lures placed in their path by the Nazi regime. Goebbels saw films as propaganda, but very subtle propaganda, he wanted to outvie Hollywood in producing lavish fun films celebrating the triumph of the German spirit, there was hardly any preaching as such in them, they were pure Hollywood escapism to distract the masses from what was happening all around them. Leni Riefenstahl illustrates the attitude of many of Marlene's old colleagues. She had been given carte blanche to produce a documentary of the 1934 Nuremburg rally and the 1936 Olympics. She used them as vehicles to portray the *Triumph of the Will,* as the title of the Nazi rally was aptly called. For her it was all angles and marching rhythms, men as personifications of power and perfect physique, it was an artist's approach which recommended itself to Hitler more than to Goebbels. Hitler personally authorised that she have access to as many resources as she needed. At the Olympics this meant there were camera crews strategically placed at each event to capture the action from every angle. It took her nearly two years to edit the miles of film that were shot. And it was a masterpiece of propaganda. But Marlene, the daughter of the military, could see the storm clouds behind all this display.The might would be used, the display was just the first part of the elaborate ritual that leads to a fight and a war.

Knowing she could have none of this, Marlene wondered briefly if she should take British citizenship, so much did she enjoy her extended stay in London during 1936. It was the location for a burning hot relationship with Douglas Fairbanks Jnr that ignited just five days after her arrival. He had to leave Claridges by the fire escape to avoid scandal after their intense and strangely poetic meetings, but they were soon photographed at all the glittering social occasions the British upper classes managed so well. The talk of the town was the unhappy King's love for Mrs Simpson. Marlene knew it was a case of an American adventuress using her sexual allure as the bait for an inexperienced and lonely man. It was obvious he was besotted. She tried to arrange a rendezvous with the king, convinced that a night with her would rid him of the ridiculous idea that his sexual needs could only be met by the American gold-digger. Marlene arranged for her car to be left discreetly at the side of the palace one night, certain that tongues would wag, but none did. She tried driving down to his home near Windsor as rumours flew about that he was to abdicate, but she was refused entry at the gates, and then the announcement came, King Edward VIII was giving up his throne for this American who so desired a royal title. But her own affair with a handsome film star, son of one of the silent era's great lovers, took up most of Marlene's time. He was eight years her junior, something she took care to conceal at 34. He himself described their nights as of a peculiar intensity. The gossips, newspapers and crowds loved the 'ideal' romance conducted amid the glamour and parties of the best houses in the land. For the rich in England, the pre-war years were one long party, none sensed the awful threat arising on the other side of the Channel. Marlene was one of the few who admitted to themselves what was to come.

In fact, the inexorable march of events towards a tragedy was vividly brought home to her shortly after they finished the filming of Knight Without Armour. In the film she played the Russian Countess Alexandra caught up in the ferment of the Russian revolution. Robert Donat, her leading man, played the part of a writer working for the revolutionaries and his assistance saved her from the death squads as they sought to leave Russia. For the part, Alexander Korda had agreed a payment of $450,000 making Marlene, as Life magazine put it, 'the highest paid woman in the world on a job basis...for taking two baths, revealing her beautiful legs and shedding a hollow-cheeked glamour through 9,000 feet of British film.'

Marlene's friendship with Alexander Korda went back to Berlin days when she had played bit parts in *Eine Du Barry von Heute - A Modern Du Barry* - and *Madame Wunscht Keine Kinder - Madam Wants No Children* - 10 years before. But Alexander Korda saw her as a way into the American market, he had a keen appreciation of her box office value, or so he thought. The film, in spite of some critical praise, did not succeed in the all-important American market, partly at least because it was too slow and long-winded. And this in spite of it being directed by Jacque Feyder, who had recently worked with the illustrious Garbo.

Alexander Korda's next project was a film of Robert Graves' book, I Claudius, with Charles Laughton in the lead part. Marlene persuaded Korda that von Sternberg was just right as the director of this promisingly decadent subject. To encourage him further, she forsook an outstanding $100,000 in fees from Knight Without Armour so that this could pay von Sternberg. But problems developed on set between Charles Laughton and the still dictatorial von Sternberg. When Hitler invaded Austria that year, von Sternberg was shocked and stunned, he suffered a breakdown, work on the film was abandoned, and for nearly a year he could speak to virtually no-one, his nervous system demanded he withdraw from a world heading towards the abyss. He was entirely right, but still few people believed what was in store.

Chapter Eleven

Lull before the storm

After what had proved a long stay in Europe, Marlene Dietrich sailed back to America in the spring of 1937 to start work on a new film for Paramount, which was to be directed and produced by Ernst Lubitsch. She was not to know it would be her last acting role for Paramount for a long time, or that it would mark the start of two years in the wilderness. The film, *Angel,* appeared to be a slick, stylish production which would employ Ernst's sophisticated talents for humour to the full, it could almost have been a film they would have made in Berlin. Neither realised it was out of sympathy with the aspirations of 1930s America, where they preferred scatterbrain hysterical comedies rather than a comedy of manners based on an old Hungarian stageplay by Melchior Lengyel.

Marlene played the part of Lady Maria Barker married to Englishman Sir Frederick Barker. On a secret visit to Paris she meets a ravishing young American, played by Anthony Halton, and conducts a clandestine affair, made more difficult by the discovery that her husband and lover served in the war together. They all meet face to face for a dinner and the plot thickens.

It was the worst film she took part in during the whole of the 1930s, and was a calamity at the box office. The Garden of Allah also failed to recoup its $1.4 million costs while Knight without Armour disappeared without trace in mainstream America. By the time Angel was released Marlene was back in Europe, on the arm of Douglas Fairbanks Jnr, making up a foursome with Rudi and Tammy. They were joined by Maria who was at a boarding school in Switzerland, and the party retired to Salzburg where they rented a chalet by the lake. For

Marlene it was a perfect break, though Douglas Fairbanks found it difficult to accept the fact that she occasionally joined Rudi and Tammy in bed to add a little spice to the evening fun, he was too American to realise that Europeans believed in showing their affections in a physical way. However, he stayed for two months or more, intrigued to be part of a *ménage à quatre*. If Rudi was happy, Marlene was happy, and Tamara, who had been part of the freewheeling Berlin café, society, went along with whatever was suggested. Maria was perfectly content to be with both her parents in such an undisturbed spot, the summer passed in a haze of golden days and loving nights while Marlene waited philosophically for the next film project to arise.

It was November before the idyll came to an end. Douglas Fairbanks returned to London, Tammy and Rudi to Paris, Maria to her boarding school in Switzerland and Marlene set out again for America. In New York she met up with Harry Edington who explained Paramount had decided not to renew her contract after the disastrous reception for Angel. There was a $250,000 payoff and that was it. She briefly panicked, rushing to Los Angeles to unencumber herself from her financial obligations. The rented house went, the chauffeur and maid, she moved into the Beverley Hills Hotel where they had a little bungalow in the garden that was allocated to her with the cost put on a long-term account. Here Marlene waited for fresh developments and made a deliberate effort to socialise with all the film people, something that she had felt little need to do in her heyday, but in Hollywood contacts counted for everything, if you were not seen on the social circuit it was soon whispered that you were a has-been. The reception of Angel was cruel from some of the New York critics, one of whom, Howard Barnes from the New York Herald Tribune, wrote:

'The production is performed with studied deliberation. Miss Dietrich is as hauntingly beautiful as ever but there is a scarcely a sequence in which one is not conscious that she is more aware of camera angles than the vitalizing of an intriguing character.'

Marlene realised immediately the fickle American public had lost some of their fascination for the old femme fatale character, as portrayed by both Garbo and herself. The woman with a past held less intrigue for an America that was at least partly recovering from the Depression years. They wanted to laugh and be taken out of themselves, not drift into the mysterious shadowy landscapes so favoured by von Sternberg. There was talk of a film in France but nothing came of it. Then an advertisement appeared in the film trade magazine bordered in red which had been inserted by Harry Brandt, the president of the small cinema theatre owners organisation. He labelled all the European imports of the early 1930s as box office poison, naming Marlene Dietrich, Greta Garbo, Joan Crawford, Katherine Hepburn and even Fred Astaire among the guilty.

She tried to ignore the ridicule, though it hurt, Douglas Fairbanks was filming in Hollywood and they conducted a very public romance, with lavish parties at Marlene's Santa Monica beach-house which she retained in spite of the economy drive. It was the perfect setting for her to invite round friends, swim nude and take in the best of California's weather. She was apparently content to wait, unfazed by the poor publicity, sure her time would come again. Reluctantly she decided to apply for American citizenship as the storm clouds grew ever thicker above Europe. But the press ad was like a death knell for her career, however hard she tried to ignore it. She had two film contracts signed, one with Frank Capra of Columbia, and one with Warner Brothers for a film called One Way Passage. After the press ad these projects were put on hold. Marlene fired her agent, Harry Eddington, and waited for the fuss to subside.

There was still time for another summer in Europe, even though the Nazi press were denouncing her, after she applied for American citizenship, for throwing in her lot with the 'Hollywood Jews'. She arranged to meet her mother and sister just over the German border in Austria but they could not see the danger of their situation when she urged them to get out of

Germany while there was still an opportunity to escape. It was the last time Maria saw Rudi's parents. Marlene brought her daughter back to America in the autumn, convinced that time had nearly run out. But the year of 1939 began peacefully enough, still no work appeared on the horizon. Marlene was helped by Rudi who had carefully placed some of the money she had been sending him all through the 1930s into a savings account.

It was possible to survive and live very well in Hollywood on the social circuit. Invitations arrived to the grandest of places, including William Randolph Hearst's palace up the Pacific Highway which was memorably portrayed by Orson Welles as Xanadu in Citizen Kane. Hearst was entranced by Marion Davis, a protégé he had discovered when she was just 17 in New York working as a dancer at the Ziegfield Follies. The unconventional relationship worked. The great driving force behind his rise to power and influence is revealed in Orson Welles' precocious masterpiece of film. It is Marion Davis, and in particular the most intimate part of her anatomy, her clitoris, lovingly referred to as 'Rosebud' by Citizen Kane. Later, when his business empire was threatened it was Marion who kept him going with the money he had previously showered upon her. They also had a daughter who was kept totally hidden away to avoid the scandal of illegitimacy. The few who knew kept their counsel, Hearst was an enormously powerful man just as the film Citizen Kane had depicted.

While no work materialised for Marlene, Douglas Fairbanks was exceptionally busy, he was an ever reliable friend and shoulder to lean on. She continued to believe it was simply a case of waiting for the right part, the right script. But when you have been dropped by one of Hollywood's all powerful studios, she discovered, your earning power disappears overnight, there were few among these latter day moguls prepared to take a chance and search outside the accepted list of current hot box office names. Marlene took stock more than once in her enforced quiet private hours. Approaching the age of 38 in 1939 she could no longer be considered for many of leading lady roles the scripts demanded, a whole new generation of actresses had arisen to claim the credits.

In June the woman from Berlin finally became an American citizen, two years after her application had been made. She could relax now that she had a base and decided to spend the summer in Europe once again, a last taste of the grand life beckoned, it helped to keep up appearances too. From then on, fate lent a hand in this summer before the storm. In New York shortly before setting sail in her favourite ocean liner, the Normandie, the pride of the French, she met up again with the German writer, Erich Maria Remarque, and the affair which had started in Vienna in 1937 took on a far more vivid life. He agreed to travel to Europe with her, although he was technically still married to his wife, Ilsa Jeanne Zambovi. He had remarried her after a divorce in 1932 so that she could gain entry to the USA from Germany. Remarque was a European cosmopolitan, like Marlene he had no time for American prudery and hysteria.

The German writer had a melancholia and sensitivity that bordered on the pathologic. But this was part of his attraction for her, a man with an ache that only love could hope to cure or at least fill the emptiness. The famous and wealthy author of *All Quiet on the Western Front* described his romance with Marlene in faithful detail in a novel he commenced that summer. It was eventually published after the war as *Arch of Triumph*. In the character of Joan Madou, Remarque portrays Marlene as he found her, while he appears as Ravic the surgeon on the run from the Nazis, a man with no papers and a past to live down. Remarque had been wounded five times in the First World War, which had produced a world weariness and cynicism, yet he was still a romantic and a poet in his inner being. Here was all Marlene wanted in a man: fierce loving attention, a sensitive refined nature, a poet, a former racing driver, a former soldier, a cosmopolitan, a collector of modern art, a connoisseur of fine wines and food. Also he had the independence that came from his book sales and the accompanying film rights. When *All Quiet On the Western*

Front was made into a film in 1930 it had generated huge business.

Remarque had followed Marlene to Paris when they first met, and then he had come to America in pursuit of her, now they were to set sail once again for their beloved Paris and the Riviera. He had smuggled out many of his French impressionist paintings to Switzerland before leaving Germany permanently in 1934 which added to his wealthy independence and stance as a disinterested observer of the human condition. But grand farce awaited them at the docks. Marlene's 34 suitcases were all loaded on board the ship when three agents of the Internal Revenue Service presented legal papers demanding back taxes on the fees she had been paid for Knight without Armour in England in 1936. They wanted an astonishing $148,000 and were not prepared to let her sail until it was paid. The arguments grew furious on the dockside. Her luggage was unloaded as the *Normandie* missed embarcation time. After Marlene called her New York attorney, the revenue men returned her luggage, then took it away again. The officers on the *Normandie* gallantly waited for film star. Finally, after an hour of argument when she would have been arrested if the Revenue people could have found a magistrate to sign the papers, they dipped into her handbag and took her jewellery: emeralds, rubies and sapphires set in gold and silver, worth by their own reckoning between $100,000 and $150,000. With this hoard of Marlene's placed in an 'escrow' account, they allowed her to sail while she vowed to get her revenge on these tormentors some day. Her new agent, Charlie Feldman, came up with the perfect counter-attack. he claimed the revenue actually owed her money because they had not taken into account her support of Rudi and his non-residence status. Eventually she did receive a credit for $23,000 and the return of her jewellery in 1941, but it was not the last of her run-ins with Internal Revenue Service, they were to be a bane for years to come, in Marlene's eyes all that she earned was hers and she spent it accordingly.

Having lived through the runaway inflation of 1920s Berlin, she believed in spending money before its value disappeared. Money passed through her hands on a grand scale. Any star is besieged by begging letters, some of which are hard to resist, and Marlene conscientiously sent off donations to good causes all through the peak of her prominence.

For what she knew to be the last golden summer, she was determined to forget the world's woes. There was nothing Erich Maria Remarque liked better than to play out a doomed romance against the background of looming, all-engulfing war, he had never emerged from the shadows of the last conflict. They knew war had to come, in Paris in June the upper classes were playing with an abandon that hinted in its desperate gaiety at the dark knowledge they all carried within their secret private selves.

One of Marlene's reasons for returning to France was more talk of a part in a French film, which Julien Duvivier was to direct, called *L'Image.* Rudi had been trying to line up the part for her from his base in the city. When Marlene joined him they mixed in the top fashionable circles, the entourage growing all the time. Von Sternberg had come for the ocean crossing as well as Erich and Maria. This party grew larger still as the hugely popular French actor, Jean Gabin, joined them in the South of France where he had a villa. His film, La Grande Illusion had been phenomenally successful. The wild intensity of Marlene's love for Erich added to her attractions for other men. But it was the secret assignations in the nightclubs of Paris, drinking Calvados, walking the empty night time streets that appealed most of all to the couple living their doomed romance. In the South they stayed at the Eden Roc Hotel on Cap d'Antibes. The party was joined by the Kennedys, who Marlene's entourage had met in Paris. She got on famously with them. Maria went swimming with the handsome young Jack Kennedy to an island where they had a picnic lunch, having carried their clothes above their heads for the swim. Marlene danced, dined and made fierce love to Joseph Kennedy, the ambassador to London, who had had a long affair with Gloria Swanson in his days as a Hollywood producer. Marlene wanted him to back a film starring the great French star, Raimu. He was tempted, but eventually nothing came of it and Marlene's financial situation became even more desperate. In Remarque's wide open tourer the couple slipped away to visit the casinos and found a perfect village hotel in Juan-les-Pins where the love affair could continue. Several times they drove all the way to Paris for the weekend, it was a secret romance amongst a backdrop of shadows, clouds, intimations of disaster and yet still nothing happened.

They lived in the moment, he drawn to a love that was given unconditionally and completely, while Marlene was drawn steadily deeper into his existential lifestyle where each day was seen as a bonus threatened by the dark forces of evil. They were moths around a flame, drawn to the brightness, knowing they could get burnt and fall to earth. Remarque became more possessive, he could not understand why she still felt attracted to other people, including Jean Gabin, another darkly burning presence that summer, while there was also a Canadian millionairess, Jo Carstairs, anchored off the coast on her luxury yacht. She was so taken with Marlene that she offered to set her up as a princess on her private island in the Bahamas. The crew-cut woman held some queer fascination for Marlene at first, she joined her several times on her yacht, but again nothing came of it in the way of backing for a film, and a film part was what Marlene desperately needed. In the midst of this dance with death, a ray of light suddenly shone through.

An old acquaintance from Berlin, Joe Pasternak, who had been about to sign Marlene for a film when she won the *The Blue Angel* part, cabled her with an offer which she considered long and hard. He had actually overseen her 1928 Berlin film *The Woman One Longs For*, so she knew how he worked. She asked to see the script. He sent advance pages of a film called *Destry Rides Again* together with an offer of $50,000 plus profit share to play the part of Frenchy, a hard-boiled saloon performer in the Wild West. It was back to her Blue Angel casting which ignored her careful cultivation in America of a different more remote image. She was intrigued at the same time as she realised how low her film stock had fallen in the two years of enforced idleness. Erich Remarque read the script and said she had to take the part. Pasternak was working as an independent producer for Universal, who were not as highly regarded as Paramount or MGM, but it was a foothold back among the Hollywood film lots. After displays of some hesitation, she arranged to sail back on the *Normandie,* leaving Erich, Rudi and Maria to follow 10 days later on the Queen Mary. Erich Remarque, mentor, lover and guiding star, had reminded her to seize each hour that was offered. Her star was once more rising in the film world, he had reawoken the Berlin actress, the natural Marlene, freed from the stifling grip of American morality with all its hypocrisies.

She understood her true strengths. When she had met the writer James Joyce the previous year and he told her he had seen her in *The Blue Angel*, she replied instantly,

'Then you have seen me at my best, monsieur.'

In the presence of genius, Marlene did not try to hide her acute self-knowledge.

Filming for *Destry Rides Again* began on the 4th of September,the day after war was declared on Germany by Britain. It was good to be back on set, and in the capable hands of director George Marshall, they proceeded at a great pace. The knowledge of the European war helped to concentrate minds, before they finished the crew were filming both day and night. After six weeks it was all in the can. The script for each day was finished the night before by Felix Jackson, another old Berlin hand, and two other writers, Henry Myers and Gertrude Purcell. Erich Remarque, who attended each day's shooting, also made suggestions which were not well received, although his situation as a refugee from wartime Europe did mean he was politely listened to.

Marlene's co-star was James Stewart, but it was she who received top billing. He had already made Mr Smith Goes to Washington which was to send him into the firmament but the film had not yet been released. They became lovers, and it is entirely possible that the man he played, the decent straightforward American, was exactly who he was. Certainly, for this picture Marlene threw off all restraints and artifices, became the floosie moll of the western saloon bars. She just pictured how it must have been in the days of the Wild West, with the excellent reference point of the dive bars of Berlin and Hamburg to guide her. Even costume was kept simple, no more than a feather boa to highlight Frenchy's feminine appeal. She was no wilting violet. The climax of the film's action was a fight with Una Merkel who played 'Lilybelle Callahan'. It was the cat fight to end all cat fights, and went on over four days of shooting. The shots of hair being tugged and pulled, of fingers reaching out to scratch and tear flesh, were all for real, it was one hell of a fight, Marlene gave no quarter and expected none. She rounded off this exhibition of female aggression with her Frederick Hollander song The Boys in the Back Room performed from the top of the saloon bar. Marlene had given the old Lola Lola a new lease of life as a western hussy, determined to get her way, who gives her life to save Destry in the final sequence of the film. It was corny, but Jimmy Stewart had been demanding all through the film that she wipe off her make-up to let out the real woman underneath. As Frenchy lay dying in his arms, she does wipe off the last of her lipstick and he kisses her on her way to eternity. The film opened on the 29th of November taking the audiences and the critics by storm. Marlene Dietrich, with her new persona, was back in business with a bang.

Frank Nugent, writing in the New York Sunday Times got it right when he said:

'Joe Pasternak has snapped Miss Dietrich out of her long von Sternberg trance.'

There was one little censorship problem, a shot of her stuffing money down her brassiere was accompanied by the line 'There's gold in them thar hills.' Inexplicably the censor missed it for the preview, but as soon as he read it in the reviews he was back for it to be removed. America might be getting closer to a full-scale war, but the country's sexual morals still needed protection.

Chapter Twelve

Wartime movies

The brilliantly opportunistic Joe Pasternak was determined to follow up the unexpected huge success of Destry Rides Again with another winner. He lighted upon a story of the South Seas, the ultimate romantic setting, except that this story involved the navy, and was to be a rip-roaring comedy. Marlene was to play Bijou, the toast of every gin-joint in the South Seas, and banned from most of them. It was Lola Lola again, but now updated to an exotic setting in The Blue Devil Café on the island of Boni-Komba (Boni was her nickname for Erich).

Frederick Hollander and Frank Loesser came up with some great songs: I've Been in Love Before and The Man's in the Navy among them. Her leading man was to be John Wayne, who had been in films since 1927 but still only earned $400 per week. His film *Stagecoach* had been made but not yet released. He was on the very edge of stardom when she was invited to check him out by the director, Tay Garnett. He was shown to her at a restaurant. She walked past, turned, looked him up and down in as suggestive a way as possible, and said to the director, 'Give me that, Daddy.'

Soon they were lovers. She adopted a straightforward approach, for he was not a man given to subtleties, Wayne played the all-American guy. On the set Marlene invited him back to her dressing room, taking care to lock the door slowly once he had entered. He smiled, sat down, acted like he wanted to be her buddy.

'Do you have the time?' she slowly asked.

'Well, huh...' he began, then stopped in mid-sentence.

Marlene was hauling her skirts up high, revealing a garter with a watch set in it. His eyes were riveted by the pale flesh shown off so well in *The Blue Angel*.

'Darling, there's no rush, we have plenty of time,' she said with even greater emphasis.

Married with a daughter he may have been, but Wayne was off his seat and into her in a trice. They knocked the dressing room around with the sheer force of their coming together, it was as though he was letting off the steam of several years of frustration, she made him feel and act like the man he was and had forgotten, he hammered her, pummelled her, could not get enough of her, she cried and swooned, which was the encouragement John Wayne needed to give a sterling performance. At last, the tryst was over, he lay back on his chair, cigarette in mouth, eyed his co-star up and down with a new respect.

They made a great team for the film. John Wayne plays Bruce, a naval officer who wants to leave the navy to follow Bijou - it was very believable by the time she had finished with Wayne and they stayed the best of buddies for the next couple of years, a brain he was not, but the deal was Marlene would teach him something about acting in return for his beefcake presence. Eventually it all ended in boredom, there was no brilliance waiting to get out of John Wayne, he was playing himself, and she gave him the belief to be himself.

As new men came into her life, some left. Douglas Fairbanks Jnr had ended their long relationship in the spring. The final straw was discovering some letters from Mercedes de Acosta, with whom she used to spend a day or a night most weeks of the year, ever since they had met in the early Hollywood days. She had joined Marlene in Paris in 1938, she was there in the background in Hollywood in 1940. The revelation of a serious contender in the love stakes, and a woman at that, was too much for Fairbanks to handle.

One night brought the situation to a head. Marlene had arranged a dinner date with him. But by the time he arrived, Mercedes had already called round and was chatting to Marlene in the bathroom while she bathed.

Douglas Fairbanks Jnr rang at the door.

'See who it is, would you Mercedes?' Marlene asked.

The diminutive Mexican let Fairbanks in.

'I'm afraid Miss Dietrich is still bathing,' she explained.

Then the phone rang. It was Erich Maria Remarque. He had also arranged a dinner date, Mercedes could not put him off by claiming she was out.

'That's not possible, she knows we have a dinner engagement, I am already on my way over.'

Mercedes left discreetly. Douglas Fairbanks opened the door to Erich Remarque , and ever the gentleman, offered Erich a drink. By the time Marlene emerged from the bathroom they were both politely sitting and waiting. She had a brainwave.

'My darlings, I have been waiting to introduce you to each other, we will be dining together tonight,' she gushed.

Then Josef von Sternberg arrived at the door and showered her with kisses. In the end they made up a foursome. Erich Remarque was used to sharing Marlene with other nameless lovers, Douglas Fairbanks less so. The break after four years of friendship happened shortly afterwards.

Seven Sinners went down well with the critics. The ever perceptive Howard Barnes in the New York Herald Tribune wrote:

'*Marlene Dietrich comes into her own again in Seven Sinners. Here you will find the tough, glamorous, eloquent demi-mondaine of The Blue Angel. If anything, she is even better than she was in that original triumph.*'

But these two Joe Pasternak successes, back to back, did not lead in any new direction. In 1941 Marlene's star began to dip again. The Flame of New Orleans directed by the Frenchman Rene Clair was a sophisticated comedy that passed over America's head.

In her next film, *Manpower,* the notorious George Raft, who was reputed to have plenty of gangster connections, played a linesman working for the Pacific Power and Light Company who vies for her favours with Edward G Robinson, a fellow linesman. She plays Fay, the hostess of a cheap clip joint in Los Angeles. *Manpowe*r ends in a terrific fight between the two buddies, by which time she has married the wrong one, it's George Raft she really loves.

In the film George Raft slaps her around. In life he tried to shock the foreign star by taking her to some lowdown dives in Los Angeles where live sex shows were performed. She thought it all rather tame and amusing compared to Berlin. Her affair with Raft finished at the same time as the filming came to an end. It had all been a little unlikely, as the critics claimed the love triangle on screen also appeared.

Two flops in a row, for her third film in 1941, Marlene was cast as Elizabeth Madden in a film which her agent Charlie Feldman had set up for Columbia titled *The Lady is Willing*. Universal were losing interest in her and Charlie seized the chance to try to work his own magic. It was a musical comedy revolving around Marlene playing a celebrated star who finds an abandoned baby and becomes determined to adopt it.

During the filming Marlelne tripped while holding the baby and had to swivel round to protect it as she fell. Her ankle was strained as a result. But with the incident filmed as it happened, it made all the papers and became big news, the story spoke of Marlene sacrificing her famous legs for a child.

Even that publicity failed to save the film. Three failures in a row, and Marlene learned at the same time *Seven Sinners* had had problems recouping its costs. By the end of the year, a black mood was coming over her which became harder and harder to shake off. War had been declared on December 7, after the Japanese surprise attack on the American fleet at Pearl Harbour, and strange fears began to cross her mind, the sufferings of the First World War were all too vivid to her, both personal traumas and the awful killing of the young men. She knew she had to do anything she could to end the war, it was the nightmare returned. Even her love for Jean Gabin could not heal the ache of being in a world gone mad again.

As one door closes, another opens. Erich Maria Remarque had been aware that she had other lovers beside himself, but he was prepared to tolerate the situation while he laboured in the Beverley Hills Hotel on his novel and she took her lovers to the bungalow in the grounds she shared with Maria. The book featured a nameless actor who beat her up but to whom she always returned, in spite of the continuing affair with Ravic, the writer's alter ego.

Rudi was in New York, having been found a job at Paramount's eastern office. Remarque depicted her as someone incapable of commitment to another person in his book, *Arch of Triumph*, which was made into a film in 1947 with Charles Boyer and Ingrid Bergman. When Jean Gabin fled Europe like so many of the refugees from the Nazis, Marlene did all she could to help him. He needed help, it was his appeal. The seventh child of theatrical performers, he had had to survive on the streets from an early age. She found him to be a sensitive man who desperately needed mothering, the true person was not the rough tough hell raiser he showed the world at large. He was possessive and violent. The assignation with George Raft was not appreciated and led to fights. Jean Gabin wanted to have a child. Most of all he fretted about his beloved France and wanted to return there from Hollywood to do what he could. Marlene found him a place in Brentwood, next door to her old rival Greta Garbo, who had not made a picture since the European war began, and there they set up home. It was an impermanent arrangement, she knew she would eventually lose him to the cause, but that too was part of the attraction.

Early in 1942 she had an abortion which developed complications and she went into the desert to stay by herself for a week, very low and depressed at this killing of his child. Then filming began on The Spoilers, the fourth remake of a classic story set in Alaska. They even had one of the actors, William Farnum, from the original 1914 film, who played a lawyer in the new production. He had been the Roy Glennister of the silent version. This part was now played by John Wayne. He has a terrific fight with Randolph Scott in the closing sequences , for it was a man's film where Marlene supplies the female interest as Cherry Malotte, owner of a gin palace in the frozen northern wastes.

'We have no brawls here, unless they're over me,' she says.

Another Wayne film followed, *Pittsburgh*, really a tribute to the mining and steel town, now giving its all for the war effort.

'It's getting so you know that where Marlene turns up there's bound to be a brawl,' wrote the New Yorker.

She plays an ex-coal miner's daughter, again being fought over by two men. It made money for Universal, but she was again typecast and in a rut. The reality of the war seemed more urgent. She felt she had to do her bit, making movies was no longer a valid response. From the day after war was declared, she threw herself into the task of raising money through the sale of War Bonds. It meant travelling around the country at fund raisers and she proved to be the most effective fundraiser of all the Hollywood stars. In clubs in the evening she put on a show and then went around the audience to get the fat cats to sign over cheques. To reward them she would sit at their tables, even sit on their laps, it was all part of the war effort. A lot of these promised cheques bounced when the time came to cash them so she devised a system with the War Bond people that she would stay at a table carousing with the punter until they had obtained clearance of a cheque. But even this work did not insulate her from the attentions of the Internal Revenue Service who made sure that her own taxes were kept up to date. She left this to her agent, Charlie Feldman, who took care of all her dues and then handed over her money. It helps to explain how she took roles got in so many bad movies around this time, her need was quite simple, to raise as much money as possible. There were the refugees from Europe to be brought over and financed.

Even in Hollywood where the war seemed far away it was not possible to insulate yourself from the horror of it all. She had helped to bring over Heinrich Mann, original author of The Blue Angel who subsisted on a pittance as a notional screenwriter. It could only be a notional position because his command of English was rudimentary. His brother, the legendary Thomas Mann, was another of the refugees, though he kept himself well away from the film people and actually wrote a masterpiece, *Dr Faustus* while located in Santa Monica. Erich Maria Remarque, another of the refugees, heard that his sister, Elfrieda, had been beheaded for daring to speak out against the Nazis. The ferocious execution took place in Munich, the very heart of the Nazi movement of evil. Remarque had become resigned to losing Marlene to Jean Gabin and he got his revenge by predicting the unhappy end to the romance in his book. In the book the unnamed actor kills Joan Madou. In life it was not so simple.

Jean Gabin found the transition to American filming tough. His two films, *Moontide* and *The Imposter* both proved a disappointment at the box office. But he and Marlene had the consolations of each other during this first year of the war. Even with Garbo next door, and film work coming in, there was an underlying emptiness knowing that they were still playing while much of the world was dying. But her war work was being noticed in some high places, in fact the very highest. While in Washington on a fundraiser, she received a message after a show to take herself off to the White House. There, at two in the morning, she was ushered into the presence of President Franklin D Roosevelt. She wondered if he had some special mission for her in Europe. He came right to the point.

'I've been hearing about your work selling War Bonds, Miss Dietrich,' he began.

'It is the least I can do,' she demurred.

'They tell me you let the customers buy your favours,' he continued.

'No such thing,' she replied, rather stung. 'I simply shower affection and kisses on them, while the cheques are cleared, what could be more harmless?'

'It's not appropriate that the United States should be raising money virtually through prostitution,' he declared, in an almost fatherly way, seeming amused at the same time as it was clear he wanted her to change her act.

She agreed.

Little did the President know how many of the actresses were offering comfort to the boys back in Hollywood. They had set up an institution called The Canteen, here troops far from home could come and have a good time, dance with the stars and even be waited on by the people they had so long looked up to. Marlene found myself dancing with boys half my age, pressing right up into them, giving them a night to remember for the rest of their lives, all too aware that they could be going to their deaths. California was the last stop before the soldiers and sailors headed out into the Pacific against the Japanese , millions of men were on the move westwards to what had been a rural part of the USA. Big defence industries were moving in, the state was being transformed into one huge armaments and military training base. There was a mad buzz in the air, excitement, fear, wild times, unforgettable nights and tearful departures as the women waved goodbye to the brave boys off to fight a war. The Hollywood actresses sought to give them something to remember of home while they were faraway. At the dockside extraordinary scenes took place as the last farewells were made, women bared their breasts in one final taunting challenge to the men's virility as they went to fight and die.

Hollywood made a film, *Follow the Boys,* showing how hundreds of entertainers were donating their services free to the war effort. The Victory Committee was made up of a whole galaxy of stars, and the film captures some of their songs, songs that were the very fabric of the nation at war. Classics like *I'll Walk Alone, I'll See You in My Dreams, Besame Mucho, Swing Low, Sweet Chariot, Sweet Georgia Brown* and many many more. Marlene's contribution was a little magic skit with Orson Welles where he saws her in half on stage. He had just married Rita Hayworth and his honeymoon nest in Nepenthe up in the beautiful wooded mountains falling down to the sea near Monterey was one of the most talked about events of the year.

But not all recipients of Marlene's fundraising efforts were grateful. One German actor, Rudolf Forster, was so disappointed with the part he was given in his first American movie that he walked off set leaving a note for the director saying he was returning 'to work for Adolf' and he did, becoming a big star of the German wartime cinema where Goebbels was spending a fabulous amount of money to maintain wartime morale.

In the spring of 1943 Marlene bid farewell to Jean Gabin on the docks in New York. She had given him all the love she could, pandering to his every need, made a home for him, welcomed him back each night by getting down on her hands and knees to worship him, change his shoes, massage his feet. She felt this need to abase herself before the men she worshipped. It could be misinterpreted. She had once been introduced to George Bernard Shaw and had fallen down on her knees before him. He, no doubt replaying his own fantasies about Hollywood actresses, had taken his penis out on the spot, she kissed it gently and reverently then hastily rose.

Jean Gabin was a jealous man, he pummelled her during the brief time she shared a house with George Raft. Unlike Erich Remarque, he could not understand her need to share herself with all those who could assist the world, with her as their ministering angel. She had little control over where her love took her, it was the only way she could help heal some of the wounds of the world. All year she had been seeing off little more than boys to the killing grounds, and now Jean Gabin was caught up in the mad rush. He set sail on a tanker to join the free French, insulted that his country, which had actually taken him to its heart only after he had wandered its streets as a teenage runaway, should be under the jackboot heel of the Nazis. One by one, Marlene's lovers departed, caught up in the war madness. John Fairbanks Jnr, Erich Maria Remarque, John Wayne and now Jean Gabin. She was beginning to feel her age, 41, though 38 according to her application for American citizenship.

The ravages of time had been held at bay by rigorous dieting, she would not eat for a month at a time, merely taking liquids. Maria had helped tape her breasts to give them uplift for the film work, while her hair, always one of her greatest assets, retained its fineness at the same time as it needed to be coaxed perfectly into place at 6.30am when she reported well ahead of time for work in the studios. Maria had become a great helper as she got older, although she had put on a good deal of weight in her late teens. Her troubled daughter had few friends her own age, though she had struck up a friendship with the young July Garland whom she had met at her Hollywood party. Marlene went dressed as the dying swan. She upstaged and dominated her daughter, but wanted to protect her as well. After the kidnap threat it was not possible to send her to school in America, instead she had tutors and bodyguards, who were her only friends. Suddenly at the age of 18 she announced she was getting married to a young actor, Dean Goodman, she had met through the Max Reinhardt school of acting, now established in California by the impresario.

Marlene should have recognised Maria's need for independence, but she could only see bounty hunters interested in rich pickings in the shape of a star's daughter. Marlene was adamantly opposed to the union. The hapless Maria had just broken off a relationship with a man 20 years older than her self, now she wanted to marry Dean. She was still recovering from an incident with her tutor, Viola Rubber, passed on to Marlene by the flagrantly lesbian millionairess Jo Carstairs. It had been a very forcible introduction to the ways of women lovers and but it took Maria years to dare mention she had been violated at the hands of Viola. Maria had an awesome innocence about the ways of the world.

Marlene arranged for Dean Goodman to be investigated. He was probably Jewish she warned Maria, only to be told by the investigator that he was a Gentile. There were rumours of him being involved with a much older woman, this too was checked out. He replied, when accused of homosexual leanings, that if this were true then why was he interested in Maria? They married on August 23 1943, neither Rudi nor Marlene attended the wedding of their chubby 18-year-old daughter. Her mother did go round to the couple's flat where she scrubbed it out completely and put in some furniture that had been in storage. She should not have worried. After four months it was over. Maria realised she and Dean had absolutely nothing in common. It should have been a warning to Marlene to let her daughter go her own way. Maria refused to divorce and insisted on remaining separated when she returned to live with Marlene. 'It is what my mother and father have done,' she told the bemused Dean. Only when Maria met the man she was to have children with did she finally obtain a divorce, after the end of the war. Her four boys were to become a joy to their grandmother in later life. As her own daughter fought to grow up, a whole new crop of women entered the cinema - Bette Davis, Ginger Rogers, Betty Grable, Hedy Lamarr, Jane Russell, Dorothy Lamour, Rita Hayworth...being the forces' favourite was the prize to aim for in wartime America, and here Betty Grable, who was one of the big contributors to entertaining the boys, emerged the clear front runner. Grable loved to travel just behind the front lines to cheer on the boys. Marlene too wanted to get close to the action, to smell the scent of battle in her nostrils, to urge the soldiers on so that the ghastly business could be over as soon as possible.

She told an interviewer in 1942, 'I want the chance to see a bit of life before I die.' She knew well enough that the Hollywood studios were not real life, it was not even a very friendly town. She wondered what to do and took herself into the desert, reinventing herself as a stage performer. She learnt how to read minds for a stage act with Orson Welles. She learnt how to wow the young boys at the Hollywood Canteen. She comforted them as they prepared to go to war. She showed not a few of them what it was to be a man.

There had been talk of a stage play on Broadway in 1942, playing in Oscar Wilde's *The Ideal Husband*. In 1943 there were long and involved negotiation about a part in a musical called One Touch of Venus where she would play a statue of Venus come to life. She went around the art galleries and museums in New York to find models for the part, dressing and undressing herself in fabulous materials for the eyes of composer Kurt Weill and producer Cheryl Crawford. Crawford, in despair that Marlene would ever sign on the dotted line, drugged her to get the signature on paper. After seeing off Jean Gabin in New York, Marlene returned to Hollywood and thought better of taking the part, pleading that the role was too sexy for a married woman with a teenage daughter. Something warned her off playing a 24-year-old.

Marlene bided her time when nothing materialised that summer. Fate again intervened. She was contacted by the one man in Hollywood who knew her from the earliest days in Berlin, William Dieterle, as he now styled himself, the same

Dieterle who had seen her audition for her first films, and had directed *Der Mensch am Wege* - 'The Woman by the Roadside' - in which she had a small part. He understood her, knew how far she had come, and what she was capable of. He had made a film of the story *Kismet* in 1920 and this story was to be reshot in Technicolor for MGM. Marlene was to play opposite the English heart-throb Ronald Colman. And she was to dance!

She struggled to find the right costume for playing the harem queen in the palace of the Grand Vizier in Baghdad. They tried gold chains, meticulously threaded by hand around her legs by two willing men as she stood legs wide apart. The censor's office ordered that she reveal a panty line to impress upon the audience that she was not naked underneath. The first day on the set the chains unravelled, breaking one after the other until she was left on set standing naked from the waist down. She walked away calmly and unconcernedly as the whole stage set looked on in amazement.

Marlene had a brainwave. Gold paint. That would solve the problem. Her legs were painted in four layers of gold, her hair was raised a full six inches in elaborate curving arches, her breasts were covered in close fitting gold cups, her upper arms were enmeshed in more gold, a loose skirt flowed from her waist, opening out to reveal the full length of the famous Dietrich legs which Wilhelm Dieterle knew had been the talk and toast of Berlin. They were to adorn a huge billboard in New York on Broadway, it was of little consequence to Marlene that she was to receive secondary billing to Ronald Colman.

The dance was her main part in a film where she only played five scenes, and four of those were for less than a minute. On the first day she performed the dance she was so bruised from all the exertion she had to take the next three days off. A double was brought in for the long shots, but the club dancer from Berlin knew how to put on an entrancing show, it was sex and legs that Wilhelm wanted, and sex and legs was what he got.

Kismet, shot in brilliant colour, with her hair radiating a golden hue from the dust she put upon it, was just the escapist fantasy and sexual release that wartime America wanted. Filming finished on the last day of 1943. The show opened to rave reviews and did fantastic box office. She knew it would, she had been going straight from the film set to entertain the boys at The Canteen and knew what effect those golden legs had had on the young men there. They were screaming and shouting for more. Marlene was back playing the role she played best, that of a real trouper.

Chapter Thirteen

Off to the battlefields of Europe

The deal Marlene had signed with MGM for $100,000 was to cover the production of two films, but with Kismet finished and no new film project on the horizon, she realised she could join the many hundreds of actors who were leaving for the war fronts to entertain the troops. Although it was considered a patriotic duty by the acting fraternity, it was not easy to join the war effort. But Marlene was determined to add this stamp of acceptability to her CV. Everyday she reported to a building in New York where she sat among the clouds of cigarette smoke generated by the long quequeus of aspirants as she waited for her number to be called. The military bureaucracy had its attractions, she became part of the group, awaited orders, her life was taken care of. Finally after long delays she was told to give an audition before a live audience of troops in Maryland. The army was not certain that the actress of a certain age was what they really required to boost troop morale. She was told to work with a troupe that included a comedian named Danny Thomas. He was an up-and-coming comic, totally unknown to Marlene Dietrich or indeed many other people, but it was Danny who rehearsed her for the live performance, the timing of the jokes, the phrasing of the songs, the projection of the voice...it was years since she had gone live in Berlin.

Danny introduced her act by announcing he had to apologise for Miss Marlene Dietrich not being there because an officer had pulled rank on him. Amid the catcalls and hisses she walked on stage in her Captain's uniform and started to peel off the clothes to reveal her stage dress which was flesh coloured and covered in tiny sequins. Danny rushed to put a modesty screen around her just in time to preserve some decorum and she re-emerged to thunderous applause as she started to sing. She had added Lili Marlene to her other standards, such as *The Boys in the Back Room*.

This song from the First World War, set to new music by the Nazi-sympathiser Norbert Schutze in the 1930s, became one of the anthems for the war, on both sides. It told of the lonely nights of fighting men, and the women who offer desperate comfort, it had all the bitter sweet sadness of war in its words and music. With Marlene Dietrich performing, the sentiments of regret and loss, sadness and resignation were all too real. She had already seen many young boys off to war while working at The Canteen in Hollywood.

The audition was passed with flying colours, but there was still the waiting for an overseas posting. The weeks turned into months. Finally in early April the troupe which included Marlene and Danny Thomas was summoned to report to the airport. It was her first flight. The cost of the insurance on her legs and her life meant that she was banned from flying by the insurers during her Hollywood career. It proved to be a very long flight, nearly 24 hours, and only when they were in the air were they allowed to open the orders and discover their destination. The sealed papers stated simply, 'Casablanca'. They had feared it might be the Pacific. By the time the plane landed, she had managed just a few snatched hours of sleep, the unheated aircraft had passed over Iceland and the polar regions as it made its laborious way to the North African coast. It was night on arrival. The officer who came to the plane was not expecting them. Eventually, he found the troupe a damp, dirty shed for Marlene's first night back in the Old World. The shows went well, the men were desperate to be taken out of themselves, forced as they were to live each day as though it might be their last. Part of Marlene's act was to sit down while playing a musical saw, when she would hitch her skirt up to reveal her 'million dollar' legs and give the troops a glimpse of what Danny Thomas called 'paradise'. That always brought the house down. Marlene revelled in her new role as sex symbol to the young soldiers.

But she was soon hurled into a confrontation with the dark forces at work in the war. She visited the hospitals and spoke to each of the young soldiers, saw the blood dripping from the bottles, felt the pathetically weak arms strung around her neck as she tried to give them hope when sadly there was often none. The amputees were always the worst, how could she promise them that everything would soon be alright? They were sad, yet brave, the wounded appreciated her visits and wept with her at the tragedy of it all. She also visited the German soldiers in these field hospitals. They knew her but could hardly believe their eyes, asking 'Are you the real Marlene Dietrich?' She was furious to see these lives being wasted away, tears flowed, comfort was given. And yet the men who had so recently been in the thick of the fighting could give her some of their energy and fierce desire for life.

Whenever Marlene went on stage, the venue erupted into a storm of noise, she stood there for minute after minute and let the animal roar of the crowd flow over her as a great wellspring of baying and howling came forth from thousands of throats, from young men far from home, far from their girlfriends.

Marlene experienced a brief flush of happiness in Morocco. The troupe gave a concert at the Algiers Opera House on the 11 April, a week after setting out from the USA. It was attended by Jean Gabin, now a tank commander with the Free French. After the show there was an air raid warning, the sky was lit by flashes of guns, and the angry sound of combat came from the darkness above. Three Junker 88s and a Dornier 217 were hunted down by the Allied aircraft and destroyed while she watched hypnotised with Jean from the balcony of their hotel, feeling no fear, it was like a movie in which they were taking part, but the deaths of the pilots out there in the night, the sweaty clammy fear generated by the hunter and hunted, was real enough. Jean and herself were in a production much bigger than themselves, their happiness could only be briefly snatched out of a treadmill of killing destined to go on and on.

The wandering group of entertainers were sent to Sicily, Corsica and the Italian mainland. There were troops all along the roads trundling up to the lines, and they gave three or four shows a day at these advance bases. The troops invariably went absolutely wild during the shows, and as they made their way there they could see the signs saying 'Dietrich, this way,' or simply a pair of legs and an arrow. Marlene played up to them for all she was worth. When she passed the troops and they looked at her, dressed in khaki in a jeep, they wondered if it could possibly be Dietrich. To settle the argument she dangled her legs out the jeep as they rode on past. That settled it, they cheered till they were hoarse.

The constant programme was beginning to affect her voice too, it began to rasp and she to splutter and cough. Pneumonia was diagnosed, she was ordered to Bari, out of the fighting line, for an intense course of the new wonder drug, penicillin. After five days she was cured of what often became a killer, Alexander Fleming became one of her pantheon of heroes, she wrote to him, sent him eggs to supplement his wartime rations and eventually met up with him when he presented her with a part of the original culture used to manufacture penicillin for the first time in 1928. It was a discovery that saved more lives than even the war claimed.

The troupe took part in the celebrations for the liberation of Rome, there were still snipers in the streets when they arrived in the ancient city by the Tiber, but the street battles had left the great treasures of Rome more or less intact, even though there were battles around Trajan's Victory Arch and the Coliseum. Marlene had already been closer to the front line than intended. At Cassino her troupe came under fire in a jeep when they strayed right up to where the combatants were contesting possession of the mountain fortress. They drove hell for leather to get out of the guns' range, Marlene had never been so afraid in her life. Shortly afterwards, an innocent break with a French actor friend, Jean-Pierre

Aumont, ended with him having to lead her through a minefield. He insisted on walking in front, Marlene gracefully let him lead her as they gingerly and with enormous care put their weight on each foot in what became a close encounter with sudden death. Enormously elated to be still alive, she breathed a sigh of relief when the troupe was recalled to New York in June. She had to fulfil her obligations to MGM by appearing at the premiere of Kismet, which became such a big hit that her reputation was restored all over again, the famous Deitrich legs were spread across huge billboards on Broadway and the crowds flocked to this rich confection of exotic colour in a black and white world. But still no second film project was forthcoming from MGM. She longed for the live audiences of brave American soldiers, and by late August was winging her way back across the Atlantic, first stopping off in Greenland and Iceland to entertain the troops there, then on to London.

She was briefly reunited with Douglas Fairbanks Jnr. The Londoners remembered her from the time of their famous affair eight years before. They even took her to her old Grosvenor Square residence, now commandeered for the war effort and part of the planning organisation. Barney Oldfield, who ran the directorate, opened all the right doors for her. She had soon met, and bedded, General Patton. She made propaganda broadcasts to Germany, as she had done on return to New York. An infuriated Goebbels had her songs banned, especially Lili Marlene, which was viewed by the German propaganda master as defeatist and anti-war in sentiment. London was swarming with troops. It was a time of total war effort, the women ran the factories and buses and played host to the near one million American troops. Marlene heard how the very ground had shook all day long as the planes left on D-Day for the long-awaited invasion, with Paris the first goal before the drive on Germany. On the fateful day for the future of Europe, Marlene had been in Italy where she announced the invasion to 20,000 men at a concert where visions of peace suddenly appeared out of the murk of chaos . Everyone there knew this was the turning point, that miraculously the end of the war was in sight.

The whole of England was one vast army camp as the British summoned up all their strength for the final battle. Inhibitions were thrown to the winds, the ever capable British women put some real backbone into both their own men and the fantastically popular Yanks. They had little money, or cigarettes, or nylons, in fact they had very little indeed except their spirit, and saw the Yanks as their saviours. The war was right on their doorstep, with doodlebugs dropping out the sky without warning. The engine suddenly cut and an explosion marked the spot it fell, often as not a shopping complex or cinema or row of houses. The great roar of the explosions echoed all round the capital, day after day, night after night. The sheer force of the blast blew in windows and doors up to half a mile away at each deadly impact. It was unnerving, but the Brits kept smiling through it all. Young mothers and children were allowed to flee to the countryside, but the great majority stayed where they were and kept the war machine humming.

Marlene's troupe was posted to France, and thanks to her connections, she took up residence in the Ritz, Paris, where she caught up with her great mentor, Papa Hemingway, war correspondent and sometime fighter with the American forces. They had been great pals since she had met him on one of the transatlantic voyages she made each summer in peacetime. She was attracted by his brain and his gruff manner. Their one night together had not worked, the great macho hero could not preform, but they stayed great buddies, something he much preferred. For all his he-man talk, Ernest Hemmingway had his sensitivities and worried about his masculinity, he had been dressed as a girl when young like her other hero writer, Rilke, and the mark never quite left him. In Paris he was in the company of a Time magazine correspondent, Mary Welsh. She had a brain, short cut hair and Hemingway's undivided attention. Sozzled together as often as not, the couple conducted a torrid affair while the war raged further up country. They liberated the Ritz's cellars and drank into the night, surrounded by generals and their staffs plotting the course of the war. But Marlene had time for diversions, one day trying to get another Time correspondent,

William Walton, into bed by appearing at this door dressed in only a hat.

'Like my hat? Cute, isn't it?' she blithely asked, but he did not bite, simply appraising her with his journalist's unblinking eye.

There was not much love lost between Marlene and Mary Welsh either, the hard-bitten journalist saw the actress as a business machine, or so she later wrote, awed by her complete command of all the details of her troupe's stage arrangements. Nothing was left to chance in a Dietrich performance.

Marlene visited the troops in Holland, where they were British, and in Belgium where they were American, then returned once more to the Ritz for early Christmas celebrations, with Papa Hemingway and Mary Welsh still encamped there. She agreed to carry Hemingway's marriage proposal to Mary Welsh which was accepted. Marlene left the new bride her bed (and some body lice from one of her visits to the front) when she was sent to Belgium again, to a place called Bastogne, in the midst of a fiercely cold spell. They were walking into the Battle of the Bulge, Hitler's last great effort to turn back the tide of the invading forces in the West which had arrived at the German borders.

The performers slept in sleeping bags in ruined houses, rats ran across the legendary face with their cold feet, the casualties mounted day by day. She worried about being captured. She could picture the Nazis shaving her head and dragging her through the streets behind some horses. She mentioned her fears to General Patton in Nancy, and he presented her with a pearl-handled pistol.

'This will do the job,' he said, matter of factly.

The man was a swaggering giant. She knew her duty and continued. But now Patton's army in the Ardennes had been trapped for a month, with casualties filling the camps. The high number of amputees particularly disturbed her. There were more than 7,000 dead, more than 60,000 wounded. Eventually they were relieved by the 82nd Airborne Brigade which fought through to the Third Army's lines. The 82nd was led by a tall dashing commander, General James M Gavin. Where Patton was brash, he was circumspect, but when it came to getting things done, the man had no equal.

Marlene's presence near the front lines continued to alarm the army since her capture would be a real propaganda coup for the Nazis. One night after the relief of Bastogne she was summoned to General Omar Bradley's headquarters in the Hurtgen Forest.

'Now that we are entering Germany, we can't let you go with the advance units,' he explained.

The man was not to be argued with. He eventually relented a little, she was to follow at some distance in the rear, and be accompanied by two bodyguards at all times. So she progressed to Aachen at the end of January and helped to organise the townspeople, giving a speech in the main street which magically cleared it for the great columns of troops and tanks passing through on their way to the forward positions. Back on German soil she was surprised to find little outward hatred shown towards her by the German people. Instead they came with their problems for her advice. The mayor offered her some precious coffee at the old cinema, now half wrecked and the site for one of the troop concerts.

'Why are you offering me this?' she asked, all too aware of how little her people had, they were starving, so desperate had their situation become.

'Because you are the blue angel,' he replied.

Even in Germany, her name lived on. It was 15 years since she had first played in Berlin. She mused on the destruction all around when speaking to a press man, he asked for her reactions.

'I hate to see ruins like this,' I replied, 'but I guess Germany deserves everything coming to her.'

That off the cuff remark was remembered long after the war in her homeland.

By March she was back in Paris at the Ritz. Patton's march on Berlin had been deliberately halted by cutting off his petrol supplies. A conference at Potsdam had decided that the Russians would be allowed to liberate Marlene's old home town, with fatal consequences for postwar Germany. But she returned to the French capital for the huge, delirious celebrations marking the liberation of Paris. She joined old friends Maurice Chevalier and Noel Coward for a spectacular show on the Champs Elysée. There was hope in the air after four years of Nazi terror and occupation. She met her saviour General Gavin at the celebrations, and they became lovers after he had taken up residence in the Ritz. Marlene learnt via Gavin's highly efficient military intelligence men that Jean Gabin's unit was in Berchtesgarden, Hitler's mountain lair. She used all her influence to get a flight there, and just as the war came to an end she was reunited briefly with him. So crazy was she to see him that she went up and down the lines of soldiers being reviewed by General de Gaulle, calling out Jean's name. The French understood and found him for her.

General Gavin flashed her a message that her sister had been located. In Belsen. The news of the death camps had quickly passed among the allied troops as they advanced into Germany and the existence of the depravities became public knowledge. She got a flight from Munich to Fassberg and was then driven 50 miles to Belsen where the head of the British unit received her in his office. He explained that Elisabeth and her husband Georg Will had been transferred to there when Goebbels had shut down all civilian cinemas the previous summer. Georg Will was put in charge of the Wehrmacht canteen and cinema for the death camp guards, which was based in the town not the camp. Marlene Dietrich asked to be allowed to inspect the death camps. The British commander, who it turned out was a Berlin Jew who had fled to England before the war, refused, but told her enough of what had been happening for her to feel physically sick. He spoke of trenches 50 metres long, 10 metres wide, that they were filling with wretched starved bodies, more than a 1,000 people a day were still dying from disease after the camp had been liberated a few days before. Her knees buckled as she took in the full evil of what had happened in Germany's name, her faith in humanity, her belief in God, were shattered. The stench of death was in the air, it was corrupting to be even in its proximity. The people claimed they had no idea what was happening, to have been unaware of the death trains passing in the night. The whole nation was guilty in her eyes. Her cause had been just. But some Germans would never forgive her.

General Gavin's intelligence units discovered Rudi's parents were held in a Czech camp, and Marlene wangled a meeting with the Russian general Zhukov to get them released. Still she heard nothing of her mother, who had been her biggest concern all through the war. There had been silence since 1938 and Berlin had taken a terrible battering from the Russians. Their troops had been given a free hand as soon as they entered German territory, German women were routinely raped wherever the Russians went.

In August Marlene was recalled to New York. She was just like the many other thousands of troops waiting for orders, some were discharged, others were being sent off to the Pacific. Then the Atom Bomb was dropped on Hiroshima and Nagasaki, the war was finally over and the implications for the world of this new weapon of mass destruction had yet to sink in.

Marlene arrived in New York with a bunch of demobbed soldiers. None of them had any money, she persuaded a taxi driver to take them to her long time favourite hotel, the St Regis, on the promise of a fat tip at the other end. Her jaw was infected and hurting, she needed some home comforts. The commissionaire at the hotel recognised her, a cheque was cashed for $100, Marlene and her GI friends took up residence in a penthouse suite. While she waited for each of the soldiers to wash and bathe, she placed a call to her agent Charlie Feldman, to get some money to cover the bill.

'Marlene, there is no money,' he announced. 'It's all gone.'

'I've just cashed a cheque for $100,' she explained, deeply shocked.

'Leave it to me, I'll think of something,' he said, hanging up.

No one wanted to know about the veterans in New York. America was celebrating the peace and the new found prosperity the huge war production had brought. Marlene took the side of the veterans when restaurants refused to serve them because they did not have ties. She despised these civilians and would continue to do so. Something had changed in her while she was away at the front.

In October, 1945, she received another message from General Gavin. He had located her mother, she was still living at the old family home where where Marlene had spent her teengage years. She immediately went to see her mother and found herself facing a woman who was much thinner they she remembered. Wilhelmine had been living on starvation rations like everyone else as mass famine swept Germany, but she was alive. Her mother held on to her Marlene's arm, upright and proud, wearing her Prussian clothes, including a tie in her blouse. Wilhelmine was tough , built of stern stuff, she faced the camera with granite faced imperturbability in spite of all she and the country had been through. Marlene caught up with old Berlin friends on her Berlin visit, people like Alexa von Porembsky who had been in the chorus line with her in the 1920s. All these old chums were friendly and welcoming, but she knew she could never return to the ruins and live there.

On the 6 November, 1945, her mother died in her sleep of a heart attack. She was 69, and had not been in good health for some time because of the privations of war. Maria Magdalena, as her second daughter had been christened, arrived just in time to see Wilhelmine buried. Now there was no home to come back to. She wept and wept.

Chapter Fourteen

The end of war

With the war finally over, *Arc de Triomphe*, the novel Erich Maria Remarque had been working on intermittently all through the war years, was published to worldwide acclaim. He sold the film rights but when it was made in 1947 as Under Capricorn, the part of Joan Madou, Marlene's transparent guise in the book, was given to Ingrid Bergman. The book revealed how Erich Remarque must have foreseen how her relationship with Jean Gabin would end.

Jean Gabin was the one man she seriously contemplated marrying, apart from the fact she still considered herself married to Rudi, and was largely supporting him. But Rudi and Marlene met infrequently. She had briefly visited California to stay with Orson Welles and Rita Hayworth after arriving back in New York from the battlefields. But little happened on the film front, apart from meeting Greta Garbo at a party Welles arranged. The Swedish star had not taken any film parts since the beginning of the war. Garbo was embarrassed by Dietrich's praise of her films and scuttled away from the party as soon as she could. She never guessed how Marlene had watched her every move all through the Hollywood years. She was determined to stay a mystery, and gradually made a fetish out of not being seen as the realisation came upon her that her film career was over in the new post-war Hollywood.

Marlene returned to France where negotiations were in progress for a film with Jean Gabin. They moved in together, spending some time in Paris and some at his farm, dilapidated from the effects of the war, in Sainte-Gemme. Like Garbo, Gabin was from peasant stock, there was an animal vitality about him which attracted Marlene, and a jealousy which repulsed her. She had to flee their hotel in Paris after he beat her so badly that she feared for my life and went to stay with her old friend Max Colpet for the night. It was the descent into violence that Erich Remarque had portrayed Joan Madou suffering at the hands of the nameless actor in his book. Even the restaurant where Joan Madou sings and drinks Calvados is based on the gypsy restaurant where Jean Gabin and she used to visit, often in the company of friends like Margo Lion from Berlin days, who was given a part in the new film.

This vehicle for Jean Gabin was titled Martin Roumagnac, although it was renamed *The Room Upstairs* for America, and had nearly 30 minutes of running time cut from it because of Catholic League of Decency objections to Marlene's character, Blanche Ferrand, a prostitute.

It proved to be a bad film. The story revolved around the character of Martin Roumagnac, played by Jean, discovering that his girlfriend was actually a whore rather than bird saleslady in provincial France. He, being a conservative builder, could not accept the situation, and kills her. But a former lover wreaks revenge in the final shot.

The reviews were bad, 'She is never false, never convincing,' said one. While another said of her wardrobe that she must be 'the envy of every bird saleslady in France.'

The reason Jean was beating her was not the poor film, it was her insistence on renewing the relationship with General Gavin. He was back in Paris, and she saw no reason to avoid being seen in public with the greatest hero, for her, of the war. She moved into his hotel for two weeks, rumour and innuendo were rife all over Paris.

'The only thing that separates Gabin and Gavin is a French letter,' said one joke doing the rounds.

The rumours proved bad for the general, his wife sued for divorce. 'I can compete with ordinary women, but not with Marlene Dietrich,' the general's wife explained. Marlene joined him for a victory parade in New York and saw how the crowds worshipped him as much as herself. She was also awarded the 'Medal of Freedom', America's highest honour for a civilian, at the wildly patriotic parade. But it was Marlene's career, rather than her insistence on retaining her personal independence , that finally brought the end to her relationship with Jean Gabin.

Paramount wanted Marlene back, after nearly 10 years away from the studio. The part was for her to play a gypsy woman who had worked against the Nazis in collaboration with a British agent, Major General Ralph Denistoun, played by Ray Milland. Marlene accepted, Jean Gabin decreed that if she returned to America that was the end, but if she stayed they could marry. Marlene walked out, by the end of the year Jean Gabin was married to a French actress. Marlene threw myself into getting ready for the new film part with her old energy, visiting gypsy refugee camps in central Europe to seek out models for her role. The whole of central Europe seethed with the millions of displaced people, while hundreds of thousands died in Germany. In France too recovery from the effects of the war seemed years away. The glitter of Hollywood beckoned, it was hard to resist.

It had been three years since Marlene had been on a Hollywood film set, she revelled in the chance to use the new European film realism in her portrayal of Lydia, a gypsy slut. She smothered herself in grease and wore rags for her part in what was to be called Golden Earrings.

'A sharp reminder of what glamour is,' said one critic on the effect she created, playing a woman who makes no bones about what she wants. Ray Milland, who did not like Marlene , comes across as a witty, polished gentleman in spite of the antagonism between the two, and the film was a great success. It was finished by mid October and Marlene took a holiday in New York before returning to Europe and France once again in January 1947. Her mother's family jewellery business had been taken over by the Nazis but surprisingly, reparations were made, and she used her former 20% interest in the business to secure Rudi's parents in their old age.

Marlene also made the fateful move into a flat on Avenue Montaigne, which was to be her home for many years. Its attraction was that it was near where Jean Gabin lived, but the break proved final. He became an obsession for her, she sat in cafés all day hoping to catch a glimpse of him when he came out of his flat with his wife. She filed away his letters in her lovers' correspondence files which was always meticulously preserved. The letters can be both painful and touching to read, as she offers to open her legs for Jean, offers herself whole and entire.

In the summer of 1947 Marlene had a visitor in Paris, Billy Wilder, who she had known in Berlin when he was a scriptwriter fresh from Austria. He had progressed to scriptwriter in Hollywood then to director and had just had a big hit with *The Lost Weekend.* He was returning from shooting some exterior scenes in Berlin for a film showing life among the ruins during the American occupation, with the black market and its values all pervasive. The stories of Berlin's women, long starved of love, affection and sex offering themselves all night for the price of four cigarettes were true, there were few illusions at war's end, and life reasserted itself even in the middle of death.

The part Billy Wilder wanted Marlene to play in *A Foreign Affair* was that of Erika von Schlutow, a German woman with a suspect past under the Nazis. She hesitated about taking the role, it got too near the truth about her life in Berlin. In the film John Lund, who plays an American Army captain, discovers that the night club singer he falls for was once the girlfriend of a high-up Nazi supporter, and had met Hitler at an opera where she was warmly greeted by him. For someone who was now firmly entrenched in the popular imagination as a vehement anti-Nazi campaigner, it could have been very dangerous to her reputation and her future career if the ambivalence of Weimar Berlin and Marlene Dietrich's values had ever become public. But the part was too good to turn down, especially under Billy Wilder's persuasion. There were details she preferred to forget about how close to the Nazis her studio boss at UFA, Alfred Hugenburg, had been. She had already seen how Leni Riefenstahl, who had been in the running for *The Blue Angel* part, and who had even visited the set the day Marlene did the famous shot astride a barrel, was now persona non grata because of her pre-war films for Hitler, even though she had never joined the party.

The film proved a big hit. Another Paramount production, it reunited her with Frederick Hollander who wrote three superb songs for her part as the night club singer, he also appears in the film as her pianist, it was almost back to *The Blue Angel* again where he is also seen playing.

Life magazine wrote:
'As a singer in the nightclub, Marlene Dietrich enjoys a triumphant return to the same sexy role that made her famous eighteen years ago in the German film *The Blue Angel* - the heartless siren who lures men to degradation and goes on singing.'

The songs, *Black Market, Ruins of Berlin* and *Illusions* perfectly capture the mood of post-war Europe. It was a cynical, world-weary, desperate time, the gloom which had settled after the devastation of the war and the subsequent shortages had produced a new bitter philosophy, but it was not so new to her. Her memories of the First World War were still fresh. There were bomb-blackened streets and houses all over the continent, few had been spared from the wholesale destruction, and the rebuilding programmes would take years to complete. Hitler had been true to his promise and fought to five minutes past midnight, she had no wish to visit the terrible scenes again of her war service.

Paris had a dark allure about it. The poet Jean Cocteau became a friend, the artists' haunts and cafés along the Left Bank seemed her spiritual home, Hollywood was just somewhere to go and earn money, not a place to spend any more time than you had to, it was too superficial compared to the realities of Paris where art and philosophy flourished in the chaos, gloom and ever present shadows of the night. There had been a film planned with the highly regarded Marcel

Carn,, who had made *Les Enfants du Paradis* during the war, but she objected to the script and more particularly her part in it. It was to be called *Les Portes de la Nuit* and dealt with Paris under the Germans.

In August of 1948 she became 'Grandmother Dietrich' making the front page of Life magazine. Maria had fallen in love with a lecturer, William Riva, at Fordham College, where she was teaching. He specialised in teaching stage design, and unlike her earlier attempts at sharing her life, this venture proved successful, producing four boys. With the proceeds from A Foreign Affair Marlene bought the couple a handsome redstone building in New York's 95th Street for $43,000 and scrubbed the place spotless, a part of her revelled in simple hausfrau tasks. In any hotel she moved into, she immediately set to disinfecting the bathroom and the toilet seat. After her cleaning sessions Marlene returned to the luxuries of the Plaza hotel still in her cleaning lady attire and asked the taxi driver to drop her off a block before the hotel, totally unrecognised by the passing crowds on New York's bustling sidewalks.

The next year she left America to film in London again with Alfred Hitchcock, who was also using Jane Wyman and Michael Wilding in star parts for a film called Stage Fright. In preparation for her part she visited Paris for fittings with Dior who provided some 'New Look' creations for her wardrobe. She also looked up Edith Piaf. This little sparrow of a woman, just 4 feet 10 inches tall like her circus performer and street contortionist father, became a loving friend. She was reputed to have had more than 200 lovers, and that does not include the women. Her life had been bizarre as well as lived in desperate circumstances. During the war years she lived in a flat on the top floor of a Paris brothel that catered for German officers. But Edith was, above all, a voice, a presence, who had suffered and survived, she was a kindred soul, who evoked all the dark passions of Paris's night time streets where human frailty is exposed. But although Edith Piaf lived for love, she said she did not have inexhaustible energy and so must restrict her friendships. She never found the satisfaction of love fulfilled. There were rumours she was frigid, certainly there was a certain protecting distance. One of her many lovers died in a plane crash. She was distraught when told just before a performance but used the occasion to go on stage and pour this grief over her audience. The public and private person fused into one. Her physical brothers and sisters numbered 17, perhaps explaining why she believed she must love so many. Sometimes in her flat there would be three lovers at the same time, she flitted from one to another as her name 'the sparrow' suggests. But drugs were what finally destroyed her. Marlene saw the slow descent into dependence and physical impairment, there was nothing she could do, she realised she was gone. Edith Piaf left this life not so long after the friendship with Marlene ended.

In London Dietrich set to work on *Stage Fright*, a typical Hitchcock thriller in which she plays an actress who also sings on stage. There are any number of twists and turns to a plot that revolves around her husband having been murdered by her admirer, Richard Todd. Jane Wyman, a big name in American movies and married to future president Ronald Reagan, plays Eve who sets out to help Richard Todd and trap Marlene. The climax comes when she gets Marlene to confess backstage, not realising that the room is bugged, with their conversation broadcast to the theatre. It is a film about disguise and furtive motives, the dark shadows in everyone's lives, it is Hitchcock being Hitchcock, one of the few directors she found it impossible to get near, there was always some reserve, it was as though he used his films to explore his own dark fears. But Michael Wilding who plays the police inspector in the film she found altogether more responsive. He became her lover and Marlene turned into a giggling schoolgirl in his presence, for he was some 12 years younger than his 47 year old co-star. He was handsome, charming, very English, yet accused her of always keeping part of herself aloof. Pleased though she was to have the undivided attention of a young English actor at the beginning of a promising career, she found herself in competition with the enemy of us all, time. Particularly in the shape of a 19 year old actress called Elizabeth Taylor.

One day Michael Wildings' visits to her suite in Claridges ceased, he was smitten by the lure of youth, rather than the experience of the older woman. Marlene stayed on in London for another month after the end of filming, spending a lot of time with Noel Coward whose friendship she had enjoyed since the mid-30s, his wit attracted her, his physical tastes were for men, so they stayed the best of friends, a situation that made few demands on her emotional life. But words could still burn into Marlene's soul, she had read the reports of Jean Gabin's comments about her, 'The old woman is too emotionally unstable.' To Marlene it was not a fault to throw oneself wholeheartedly into a relationship. But family, she believed, is what endures. She returned to New York where Maria was now expecting her second child and became the proud grandmother again, taking her first grandchild for walks in Central Park, scrubbing out Maria's apartment from top to bottom and losing herself in simple physical tasks. Maria had finally managed to get a stage part and her mother was proud of her, she had for many years been her confidante and adviser, often accompanying Marlene to select clothes which were made up by the world's top couturieres. She overlooked no detail of these fabulous creations, asking for and eventually receiving perfection. She believed a star can only preserve their image by looking immaculate beyond the dreams of ordinary people, even if it requires a superhuman effort to create the illusion. Maria's entry into the theatre was with old silent movie star, Tallulah Bankhead, in a Broadway production of Foolish Nation. She had, of course, been offered the part through her connection with a legend, but her name as Maria Riva offered few clues to this for those not in the know.

In New York the big sensation of the year was the stage play The King and I with a former director turned actor in the lead role, Yul Bryner. He was Siberian and had shaved off his thick black hair to create a new look of mongoloid ferocity and intrigue, it suited him so well that he remained lockless ever afterwards. Marlene was irresistibly attracted to his muscular lithe frame, the 20 year age gap melted away, their romance became the talk of the town, making a suitable contrast to Life magazine's continuing portrayal of her as the world's most glamorous grandmother. With no film parts in prospect it was increasingly necessary to continue acting the part of the star. An opportunity occurred in Los Angeles when she was invited to present the Oscar for the best foreign film. She did her homework very thoroughly, checking out from all the dress designers she knew what the women would be wearing at the presentation ceremony - all Hollywood would be there in the 2,800 seat auditorium. The trend was to wear glamorous sequined creations with flouncy ballroom dresses, so she selected a slinky black dress down to her ankles, the only unusual part of the outfit being that there would be one deep split past the knee to reveal the fabled legs. Marlene even checked out which side of the auditorium she should enter from so that the split - and the legs - caught the audience's eye.

No one remembered who won the Oscar but they all remembered the dress and the entrance. None realised more than Marlene that every public appearance of a star is a performance that creates the stuff of legend. Fortuitously this high visibility paid off, she had an offer of a film part from Henry Koster who had worked with Joe Pasternak in Berlin as a very young assistant. He wanted her to play the part of a star in a film called No Highway starring James Stewart who she had last worked with in *Destry Rides Again*. The film was to be made in England and she plays Monica Teasdale, a famous English actress flying across the Atlantic with plane designer James Stewart. He is convinced that metal fatigue will cause the plane to crash after 1,420 hours in the air. His calculations prove wrong, 'I guess you multiplied someplace where you should have divided,' she says at one point, but he convinces her he knows what he is talking about and lends her authority to his warnings of disaster if the plane is allowed to take off from Newfoundland. He has forgotten to include air temperature in his calculations, but it is only a very temporary reprieve.

This is the one film when she plays her modern self, the next film offer she had was more predictable still, it was a western with her playing a version of 'Frenchy' from *Destry Rides Again*.

The offer came through her old friend (and brief lover in the early 30s) Fritz Lang, who had made his name in German cinema with classics like *Dr Mabuse* and *Metropolis*. She should have known that a western with humourous overtones was not really his forte, and although her fee of $110,000 was persuasive there was little left over for the sets. The film was one of her rare ventures into colour, and she became one of the most glamorous and stylish females from the days of the Wild West. For in *Rancho Notorious* she plays Altar Keane, an ageing bar-room queen who has set up a ranch where various desperadoes can hide out in exchange for a cut of the loot. The unspoken rule being that no-one can ask any questions. This arrangement is interrupted by a man seeking the killer of his fiancé,, who befriends her in his search to find the truth. Marlene recreates her old bar-room days in a series of flashbacks, the great attraction of the film for her. Its one high spot proved to be where the women ride the men bareback across the bar-room floor. But Fritz Lang's direction was heavy handed, his style relied too much on the old silent melodramas rather than fast action and repartee. He had persuaded Howard Hughes to finance the film, but it was one replay too many of old times.

Long before they finished filming Fritz Lang and Marlene Dietrich were no longer talking. He did not take kindly to her suggestions, 'I am Lang, not von Sternberg,' he angrily exploded one day. But he had learnt Joe's exacting ways, it was a pure kind of sadism, forcing her to replay a scene time after time, which under his demonic gaze forced her to freeze up when she should have been relaxing. A stilted Marlene appears on screen, she knew it was going to flop, but not how badly. Or what effect it would have on her film career. Lang was determined to offload the blame. He accused her of having lost herself in a portrayal of a movie star.

'If a dog walks into her dressing room, she'll start acting,' he claimed.

Of her love life he did know some details. He had not forgotten how in the early 30s she had picked up the phone after they had made love, to ring another admirer. It was a brief relationship. Now he accused her of always seeking the perfect man, doomed to never be successful and so moving on to the next affair. The legend had attracted him until they finally worked together when there could be no more pretence. they could not share their fantasies.

But Rancho Notorious did mark a new beginning for Marlene. As part of the publicity for the film she sang *Falling in Love Again* live before the film opened in the cinemas, starting with Chicago in early 1952. This was followed by more of her songs from the occasional recordings she had made of numbers like Lilli Marlene. The live performances went down fantastically, the legend lived on independently of the actress Marlene Dietrich. It was to take some little while for her to appreciate the fact, but a new career was beckoning just as the film world was losing interest. The brief resurgence of fame that came from Billy Wilder's and Alfred Hitchcock's films had subsided. In Hollywood it's rare to make a comeback, she had done it twice already but was aged 51 at the end of 1952.

Chapter Fifteen

Marlene Live

Just as Marlene Dietrich was appreciating how badly *Rancho Notorious* was to be for her film career, her daughter Maria's career as a TV actress started taking off. She appeared in several long running soaps, which did not produce much income, but her mother made sure the couple had a supplementary source of funds. Maria's new TV connections also proved useful. Marlene set about developing different sides to her show business career in New York while the film world went through changes, not least because of the impact and challenge of TV, but the flickering TV screen was too small and low key to appeal to the movie star. She, like few others, appreciated the hypnotic effect of a screen large enough to fill an audience's vision. One of her successful diversifications was into radio, which perfectly suited her husky voice, 'a voice that could break your heart' Hemingway called it. The effects of constantly smoking were also beginning to roughen the sweet angelic yet mischievous tones with which she had first spoken and sang in *The Blue Angel*. The setting for the weekly radio series was called Café, Istanbul where she introduced a quick moving selection of songs mostly sung my her. It was modelled on *Casablanca*. Not surprisingly, because the writer was Murray Burnett whose unproduced play Everyone comes to Rick's was the basis for the phenomenally successful film that had perfectly caught the atmosphere of the war years with its fast moving plot and hard bitten characters, moved almost in spite of themselves to take the side of the angels when the chips were down. Marlene called myself 'Madamoiselle Madou' after Erich Remarque's name for her in *Arc de Triomph*. The shows enjoyed two 13-week runs on ABC. Then Marlene moved to CBS, called herself Diane La Votle, and the show *Time for Love*. She also made some recordings of her songs from *The Blue Angel* days onwards. What her voice had lost in freshness it made up for in its knowing world weariness and hints of unspeakable sadness. The record was released in both German and English to popular acclaim, becoming a hit on both sides of the Atlantic. Always believing in keeping busy, Marlene also wrote some short stories that she showed one day to Dorothy Parker, who claimed she was impressed. There were articles for the women's magazines, good homely advice dispensed in such pieces as *How to be Loved* for the Ladies Home Journal.

But none of these outlets for her talents seemed likely to generate the income Marlene needed for all her responsibilities. She knew she had to keep a high profile. When Maria mentioned a charity affair at Madison Square Gardens on behalf of children with cerebral palsy, Marlene offered her services to the organisers. The theme was to be built around a circus performance, and most the stars in town volunteered to take part. Marlene thought long about how she could create an impact and came up with a new image for Dietrich, that of Master of Ceremonies. She dressed in some short black pants, set off by long black boots with gold bands, a short scarlet jacket, a black top hat and, as a final touch, she carried a whip. It was a recreation of the female dominatrix figure so familiar to her from Berlin's streets, not that the Americans ever twigged the sado-masochistic undertones. But the performance, which was rounded out with some songs, drew rave reviews from the New York papers. One of those who saw the show was Bill Miller who ran the Sahara hotel in Las Vegas. He remembered the bravura performance and later gave her a call.

Would she perform her songs in his hotel? he wanted to know. Marlene demurred. He mentioned the salary, $30,000 a week. She accepted. At exactly this time Rudi was rushed into hospital for an operation where half his stomach was removed. He was a sick man and would not be able to work much any more, in fact he had been doing little work with the film office for a long time. Tamara was also reported to be fraying at the edges, her mental health was so delicate that it was recommended she go into an asylum. But Rudi resisted. He wanted to start a chicken farm in California, a friend lent him $10,000 for the down payment on a one and a half acre farm in the San Fernando valley and he and Tamara went to live there. At first Tarmara's stability improved and Rudi seemed happy to be among his chickens. Marlene arranged to pay his mortgage and he and his Russian companion retired into obscurity.

It was December before Marlene's show opened at the Sahara, but by that time she was ready for the new Dietrich to be presented. For the occasion she had three fabulous dresses made up which were to cause a sensation. Never has so much work gone into a dress creation. It required her to fly to Hollywood from New York and stand there for 10 hours at a time while each sequin and rhinestone was sewn into position. She was an expert seamstress herself, so she knew what she was talking about when she decided where each of the hundreds of sequins should go. $8,000 went on the dresses. The intended effect was that she should look naked from the waist up, with the sequins placed at two strategic spots upon the open net of the upper part of the dress. In reality, she wore a figure hugging foundation garment that was flesh coloured from neck to crotch, but few ever knew her secret. A 52-year-old woman dare not rely on nature alone for her effects. And in the Dietrich legend she was ageless, still a haunting figure beyond the dreams of men...and women.

The show only lasted half an hour, but the preparations for it went on for months. At last she could control the lighting, the programme, the entrance, the exit, the musical arrangement, it was her own show rather than the regimentation of the film world. She was dependent on no one but herself for success, the way she liked it. When the stage lights picked her out in her shimmering creation, she brought the room to a hush. Strict orders had been given that no one could take their place after the show started, and no orders could be given to the waiters while she performed, all attention had to be on the singer. She launched into her first song after simply saying 'Hello', very slowly, while dazzling and feasting their eyes. Then she half spoke, half sung the words rather like her friend, the *diseuse* Edith Piaf. The words took on deep meanings, they were meant to be heard and do their work, she always believed in the power of poetry and knew many of her favourite poets' works by heart, so that by the time the last number came up - *Falling in Love Again* - she held the audience's emotions totally captive. The illusion of a half naked Dietrich on stage, swathed in glittering sequins, wearing a long cape trimmed in black fox, fixated the Las Vegas crowd, who were in reality simply taking a break from the gaming tables. But she had held the attention of far more difficult audiences in the Berlin clubs, all the old tricks and some new ones came into play for the perfect performance. A new Dietrich was born, the old film actress was replaced by a living legend, who sang for her supper. There was a lot of comment in the papers about how shocking and indecent her outfit was, which did the legend no harm whatsoever. After the three-week show she was booked for the following year and there was talk of taking the show to London, which was arranged for the summer of '54. Although at only half the salary offered in Las Vegas, it still made her the highest paid live entertainer in the world. A new career had begun and Marlene was happier than for years with the chance taken out of her earnings capacity.

She loved the lights, the razzmatazz, the hustling crowds who sought instant happiness on the gaming tables, it was like the Wild West of old and was indeed run by Mafia connected gangsters. They had taken a small town in the desert and turned it into a gambling paradise helped by some lax local laws. These men were powerful, you crossed them at your peril. Marlene had some problems with studio boss Harry Cohn, at Columbia, who had been talking about Marlene appearing in a musical with Frank Sinatra and a new face, Jack Lemmon. She told him that Lemmon, who she knew nothing about, was not right as her co-star and turned him down for a film that what was to be called Pal Joey, a monumental flop. Cohn was livid with rage at this snub but Marlene had simply overplayed her hand trying to name her co-stars, even though the power to approve co-stars was in the contract. Marlene had made sure that everything went into a contract. She then tried prevailing on Harry Cohn to let her use Jean Louis, the studio's chief wardrobe designer, to create her stunning Las Vegas outfit, only to be turned down flat. But she was utterly determined, she had seen the outfit he had designed for Rita Hayworth in Salome the previous year, and that was what she had to have. She talked to the management of the Sahara and a call went up from the hotel management to Chicago and then down to Hollywood. When Harry Cohn got the call from the mobsters he changed his mind very quickly indeed. There was a tale of one producer, who had tussled with the mob, waking up in his bed with the head of his favourite horse lying beside him. Actors like George Raft made a point of hanging out with the mob in real life as well as on film. Compared to the black marketeers and fat cats of Berlin just after the First World War they were pussy cats, there they had calmly driven past thousands of people starving on the streets in their luxury limousines, completely indifferent to the suffering. A part of Marlene even then had vowed she would one day be on the rich men's side of the great divide between poverty and wealth. She enjoyed her success in Las Vegas, it had been a long journey.

London was even more of a dream. The show was booked for the Café de Paris with the opening at midnight. All the top people in show business and society were there from the Queen's sister, Princess Margaret, downwards. Noel Coward, who met her at the airport, introduced her on stage at the night spot in Leicester Square, and for the more conservative tastes of London she made some changes to her costume. There was a silk lining to the previously see-through netting across her front and breasts, (these 'heavenly spheres' were much admired in the press, little did they realise how sticky tape was used to keep them upright). Marlene arranged for an entrance coming down some stairs where yards of chiffon was blown upwards by a fan to reveal her legs, in an anticipation of Marilyn Monroe's manhole cover shot . Marlene stayed at the Dorchester in a palatial suite with a golden bed and a golden bath until at 10pm she left for her midnight opening. The reviews of the show were ecstatic.

'The purr of the sacred cat,' wrote the News Chronicle, while a young critic, Kenneth Tynan, claimed to hear a voice hinting of leather and secret sexual knowledge, 'the seductive whisper of the murderess', he wrote. Marlene provided a sexual cocktail and it produced the desired effect. Although keeping a little distance, at the same time she seemed so near to the audience. For the austerity ruled British it was sexual arousal on a grand scale. The six-week show was a sell-out weeks before she arrived. The post-show highlife was fabulous, just as she remembered it from before the war. As often as not it was past dawn by the time she got to bed and mid afternoon before she rose. Little did anyone realise that the ageless Dietrich, living proof of the defiance of time, had had a second face lift that spring which helped to explain the rather fixed cat-like expression on the face of the performer. But Noel Coward in his introduction, called her simply 'our legendary, lovely, Marlene.'

By the time she returned to Las Vegas, she was an established cabaret performer who could command her own price. The legend had acquired a momentum of its own. Yul Bryner was in the audience for one of her shows, even he could not resist the lure of the bright lights and stardom though he knew the person behind the legend. She was determined to fight the encroachments of age, taking a lover half her age, the handsome beautiful Eddie Fisher. He joined her long list of conquests in New York. She asked him to pop by when he was in town after meeting him in Vegas during her first show. He became a devoted admirer after sampling the delights of her bedroom with its mirrored ceiling. At 25 he was destined to become another husband of Elizabeth Taylor who Marlene grew to hate, for another conquest, Michael Todd, also became a husband of the English star. Todd, a consummate producer, was putting together a film of Jules Verne's novel *Around the World in 80 Days* in which he wanted to use 'name' stars in cameo parts. He contacted Marlene to play a dance hall queen in San Francisco, with Frank Sinatra as her accompanist on the piano. George Raft was also there with Red Skelton in the same scene. Her best line in the film is where David Niven's manservant comes into the club.

'I am looking for a man,' he says.

'So am I,' she drawls back.

The picture went on to win the 'Best Picture' Oscar. Apart from a nomination for her performance in *Morocco*, the Oscars never figured in Marlene Dietrich's long *curriculum vitae*. But then she never believed in playing parts far removed from the real Marlene, cripples and waifs and strays were not her forte. They would have affected the legend's all pervasive image of untouchable unreachable glamour. More to her liking was a film part offered to her in 1956, an Italian production called *The Monte Carlo Story* where the male lead was the Italian heart-throb, Vittoria De Sica. Filming was on the Riviera so she simply relived the glorious pre-war days with Erich Remarque, the Kennedys and Jean Gabin. In reality the film was going nowhere, it was meant to be a vehicle for Vittorio who had made the hit, *The Bicycle Thieves*. However the story of two high spenders down on their luck, and fooling each other about their bank balances, was a one-joke story, which could not be rescued by beautiful photography of the Riviera. Marlene started to act temperamentally in the filming of what she sensed to be a flop. She became impossible, throwing a tantrum when the hotel presented her with a bouquet of a dozen roses after she had complained at their lack of attention.

'You call these flowers, I want 5,000 roses,' she screamed at the management.

They promptly returned with bouquet upon bouquet of flowers, while she managed to virtually take over King Farouk's yacht which the film company had hired for the duration of the film.

With her new role as chanteuse in the world's top night spots Marlene knew she had no need to pursue film parts, so it was some surprise when another film offer came up through her old friend, Billy Wilder. Called *Witness for the Prosecution*, it seemed a variation on *Stage Fright*, her last big success. The complicated plot line revolved around her role as Christine Vole accusing and implicating her husband in a murder during a courtroom drama. The twist was that as she was married to him and was not allowed, in law, to implicate him in the murder. Christine Vole had a past, as a German entertainer at the Red Devil club. At the denouement it is revealed that she was already married before she became Mrs Vole and therefore could testify against her husband. An anonymous phone call from a Cockney woman (actually herself in heavy disguise) reveals her secret past, and her testimony is discredited. Her husband goes free.

The triumph of Marlene's double role, especially as the Cockney woman, could not be revealed to the press because it would spoil the plot for the audience. it was even more galling because the film went on to win most of that year's awards. Billy Wilder made it even more difficult for the truth to be told by saying that the scene had been shot twice, with Marlene taking the part of the Cockney woman once, and a double doing the second take. Charles Laughton, one of the film's stars, had coached her to get the accent almost perfectly right, but no one was allowed to be told. She had to be content with reviews such as the following:

'Marlene Dietrich proves in Witness for the Prosecution that she is a dramatic actress as well as a still glamorous chanteuse'.

Billy Wilder won a nomination for best direction while Charles Laughton and his wife Elsa Lanchester were nominated for best actor and best supporting actress. Marlene had to content herself with the thought 'What does it matter what you say about people?' the end line of a much under-rated film she had just completed with the great master, Orson Welles, A Touch of Evil. Her part in this was small, just four or five scenes that were all filmed over a single night. She plays a fortune-telling madame in a bordello owned by Orson Welles. At one point she gazes into her crystal ball and tells him 'Your future is all used up.' Marlene is dressed in a dark wig with smouldering eyes, all too aware that he will die before the night is over. For the night's work, and the two days she spent trawling for her own wardrobe in the junk shops of Los Angeles, she received $7,500. It proved to be one of Orson's deeper films, probing the nature of good and evil, but that realisation only occurred to the critics long after it was released.

So although she had two films released in 1958 virtually back to back she knew that her career was that of the nightclub entertainer. So successful was the show that it was booked all over the world. By a happy coincidence she had taken on a fresh lease of life thanks to a new musical arranger. The way she acquired him was strange and magical. Noel Coward, who had strongly advised her against taking the job in Las Vegas, had been bowled over by her success, so much so that he took up an offer to appear there himself. When he engaged the services of Marlene's musical arranger, Peter Matz, she was incensed at the cheek of her old friend. Peter Matz, apologetic but unrepentant, said he would arrange a replacement just as she was flying out to Hollywood to stay at the Beverley Hills Hotel. She thought no more about the promise and left town. Hardly had she arrived at the hotel when there was a knock at the door. Peter Matz had left a message for composer, Burt Bacharach, who had picked it up at LA Airport on his way through town. He came round to the hotel immediately to see Marlene, and they instantly clicked. He was 30, charming and eager to please. He was engaged by a woman nearly twice his age on the spot. The definitive Marlene show took form with Burt rearranging many of her songs to fit the new idiom of big band sounds. For the next few years they were to travel the world together.

The ballyhoo that the world show generated was not all left to chance. They had three shows in South America. Marlene arranged for a hired crowd of fans to mob her at the stage entrance in Buenos Aires, having taken the time to visit the local police station in the afternoon to ask for protection. All they offered were some off-duty policemen who she had to hire. And so it came about that America's press carried a picture of Marlene being carried over the heads of the mob, having 'fainted' in the crush.

They took the show to Paris in late 1959. For the grand opening there was a star-studded audience including Orson Welles, Margo Lion, Jean Cocteau (who was to die within a short time on being told of the death of Edith Piaf) and the French actor who she had walked through a minefield with in Italy, Jean-Pierre Aumont. Paris was taken by storm, Burt Bacharach persuaded her to take the show to Germany the next year. She hesitated, he proved all too persuasive, a series of shows were booked across Germany beginning in May 1960, 30 years almost to the day that she had sailed for America after the opening of *The Blue Angel*.

The theatre they chose for the first performance was the rebuilt Titania Palast in Berlin. Ticket sales had not gone too well, although they were asking top prices, so to boost attendance they distributed many free tickets until nearly all the seats were taken. A full scale furore had been whipped up in the German press, the least unpleasant charge made against her was of her being a traitor who should leave the country immediately. On the Sunday before the Tuesday opening, a paper obtained her birth certificate, triumphantly announcing she had been born in 1901 rather than 1904 or 1906 as she liked to claim. It had always been difficult to explain Maria's age and had resulted in Marlene saying both herself and her mother had given birth at the age of 17. On the subject of her opposition to the Nazi regime she gave not an inch. Willy Brandt was part of the audience for her opening night, and on her arrival in Berlin she had arranged that old friends like Berlin and Hollywood film director, Wilhelm Dieterle, should be there to greet her. The mood was hostile from the German press from the moment she arrived. They wanted her back in America, old wounds smarted.

On the night of the opening, she arranged for the car to drop her off several blocks before the Titania Palast, so that she could walk. These were her streets, her people, this was her city, even if 30 years had passed and there was barely a building standing from when she had lived here. There was speculation she would be pelted with tomatoes and eggs. 'Not eggs, I hope' she joked, 'you just can't get rid of the stains.'

But the crowds parted for her as she drew near the theatre. A woman in a scarf and dowdy coat pushed her way through to Marlene. She kissed the star. 'You're still one of us,' she said amid tears. Marlene cried, gave her a great big hug and pushed on to a show where there were 18 curtain calls. She faced down the Nazis and their sympathisers, showed them the true German spirit. By the time the show reached Munich there were 64 curtain calls and Germany was hers once again. But she could never go back, she realised, the spirit of the country had changed.

Chapter Sixteen

Judgment at Nuremburg

Marlene Dietrich thought her time in films had come to an end, but in 1961 came what was to be her last role of major importance. Directed by Stanley Kramer and written by Abby Mann it was to win many of the Academy Awards the following year, including best performance for Maximillian Schell as the prosecutor, and best script for Abby Mann. She plays a part very close to her own circumstances as she had done all through her film career, there was little to separate the actress Dietrich from the flesh and blood Dietrich. Her role is that of the aristocratic wife of a Nazi general who is dead but she finds it difficult to admit her husband did any more than his duty. Her scenes act as a relief from the tension in the courtroom where the story focuses on four lesser known defendants from the array of Nazis on trial for complicity in war crimes. Spencer Tracy plays the judge who stays at her home during the trial, and he was also nominated for best actor, while Montgomery Clift was nominated for best supporting actor, and Judy Garland for best supporting actress.

The three-hour film examines the nature of Nazism and how it held such sway over the German people. Marlene's character, Mme Berthold, is from an old German family, who can see the terrible things done in Germany's name, yet still holds to her belief in German customs. Hitler was not part of that tradition. As Marlene knew back in Berlin in the 1920s, they were never more than violent thugs and criminals who had been of little consequence until UFA's film boss, Alfred Hugenburg, had begun putting huge amounts of money into the party as part of his dream to revive the old traditional German values. But the Nazi party had used to money to install themselves in an impressive palatial headquarters in Munich and set their own agenda which the big industrialists wrongly thought coincided with their own. The Depression did the rest, the crowds of unemployed shopkeepers, clerks, small people, bitter people, frustrated people, swelled their ranks. Only the peasants and the farmers firmly resisted the Nazis, in the cities they bullied their way into prominence until the few in high office who stood up to them were murdered and beaten up by the hired gangs.

Mme Berthold, and Marlene, wanted the world to know there was another Germany, a nobler Germany, but in the aftermath of the war there was too much hatred to expect the victors to allow that. As her tour of Germany had shown her the Germans no longer spoke the same language, and for all the praise garnered on the tour, it was the insults she remembered, the woman in Dusseldorf who screeched 'I hate this person who betrayed Germany in the war,' as she spat in my face. Marlene should have paid more attention to the accident in Wiesbaden when she had toppled off the stage and broke a collarbone. It was a sign that her bones were becoming weakened, and this may have been connected to her privations during the First World War when she was an adolescent girl living on starvation rations. Age was pressing in on her, there was been another facelift before the film, which increased her mask-like appearance, though if anyone guessed the reason none commented. She began visiting a clinic in Switzerland where Dr Paul Niehams was offering rejuvenating treatments using lamb essences administered with a syringe.

Another film opportunity intimately connected with her German heritage came up at the end of 1961. It was a documentary directed and produced by Jack Le Vien, called *The Black Fox,* which narrated the life of Hitler and showed the gross excesses of his regime through the analogy of a mediaeval tale of Reynard the Fox. Along with the new documentary film material which the Americans unearthed, there were shots in the documentary of the hideously ugly caricatures by returned soldier and artist George Grosz who mercilessly portrayed the human failings of 1920s Berlin, as he portrayed the degradation seen on the streets with shattered war victims selling whatever they could to scrape a few pfennigs together. Marlene remembered it all vividly. The men selling matches on street corners. The women selling their bodies. Had she not herself worked in a roadside kiosk in her early 20s to simply survive?

Marlene's job was to read the commentary which she did in a totally professional, factual and unemotional way, there was no need to embroider the facts so stunningly being revealed on screen. The general public were still generally unaware of the gross excesses of the Nazis. Jack Le Vien spared no punches. The film closed with shots of the concentration camps. Marlene had seen the smoke still ushering from the chimneys at the war's end in Belsen. She had smelt the flesh burning. Her narration ends, 'And the children, they didn't even spare the children.' It was her own very special condemnation of both Hitler and many of her people.

If she had had any doubts about her wish to bring the war to an end as soon as possible, these images settled the question. But what is less generally realised is that she comforted German soldiers in the field hospitals as well as the Americans and British. She showed no favouritism among the unfortunate, she was there to tend wounds, not inflict them. just as her songs were to heal souls, not inflame them.

While her film work was nearly over, the world was her oyster in the early years of the 60s as Burt and she took their unique brand of show to the great entertainment capitals. To the Sahara in Las Vegas at the end of 1961, to the Olympia Paris in spring 1962 for a huge success. The sense of triumph was helped on its way by her instructions for flowers to be placed at key points in the theatre so that admirers (who were hired) could throw them on stage during the standing ovations. These she loved, they were her physical contact with her fans, the visible proof of their affections. Indeed, she recorded them and played the ensuing record to anyone who would listen in her dressing room and during social evenings. Noel Coward was dismissive, but for Marlene the performance was everything, why she had to go on even as she entered her 60s.

There were fresh fields to conquer. They took the show behind the Iron Curtain to Poland, where she let the students persuade her to join them for a party after the show and perform her songs round the piano, for the price of some Polish drink. The young actors fell in love with her, life took on more of a Slav aspect, she always claimed to have a Russian soul. The top Polish actor, Zbigniew Cybulski, came to see her off at Wroclaw station, her party just caught the train in time as they departed at midnight amid showers of kisses between Marlene and her new admirer. The young man was to die a few days afterwards when he tried to jump aboard the same midnight train to Warsaw as it was leaving the station and fell under its wheels. Marlene sobbed bitterly on hearing the news in Moscow where she met the young poets like Yevgeny Yevtushenko as she took the city by storm. She and the Russians were allies against Fascism and they took her as a kindred spirit. In Poland, her song *Jonny* climbed to the top of the hit parade. After this glorious new experience behind the Iron Curtain where people knew none of her films but many of her songs, she returned to London for a show at the Queen's Theatre in December 1964. The previous year she had been in London town for the Royal Variety Show, on the same bill as the newly emerging Beatles. But this time it was her own show pure and simple.

The critics raved. Harold Hobson from the Sunday Times wrote of 'a mysterious passion, a controlled intensity of emotion dearly brought back from the gates of hell'. While the acclaimed theatre critic Kenneth Tynan succinctly wrote *'She knows where all the flowers have gone'*. In England the war may have been over for nearly 20 years but it was still vividly fresh for the people, still a source of pride that they had overcome what seemed impossible odds when they stood alone against Germany.

Marlene's own personal battle awaited her after this triumph. In January 1965 she was diagnosed as having cancer of the cervix. For some time she had been noticing a little bleeding but had not worried too much about it. She thought it connected to the menopause perhaps. But Maria in whom she confided was insistent that she see a specialist. Maria was now old enough to stand up to Marlene's displays of truculence. She had moved to London in 1957 with her four sons, and the youngest, John David, was born there in 1960. They were a source of joy and strength for Marlene, entirely separate from the world of theatre and cabaret but there for her whenever I wished to take her place at their table. They were one of her reasons for continuing to work as she often told them, but there was very little for the old trouper to do except perform. With Burt Bacharach at her side, there had been a late flowering of her cabaret skills, he had brought them to a fine pitch and perfection. However, when she went to Switzerland for treatment of cancer through radium implants, he began to see Angie Dickinson a young actress who had caught his attention. The fateful parting of the ways came at the Edinburgh Festival in 1965. She was devastated, he was to be her last long-time lover, after the cancer treatment sex was painful. More sadnesses crept into her life. News came from California that Tamara had been murdered in the asylum she had entered. She had died at the hands of one of the patients so little could be done to exact punishment. Rudi had been devoted to her for almost as long as he had known Marlene. Tamara had been his prop, his ego booster for so long, and now that was gone, there was little for him to live for except his chickens, which were flourishing on his San Fernando valley farm, he had as on so many occasions proved everyone wrong in their predictions of the enterprise's failure.

Marlene's main companion was her secretary Bernhard Hall, an English dancer who she recruited out of her supporting dance troupe in 1957. He took care of all the arrangements on the tours. Together they visited Rudi on his farm for two weeks. They saw Tamara's grave just outside the Paramount film lot. Bernard Hall said he found Rudi the sweetest man he had ever met. Marlene suggested he get into Rudi's bed, which he did, but nothing happened. Rudi was not that way inclined.

They left Rudi to his chickens and the tour continued around the world. There were shows in South Africa where she objected to apartheid segregation of the races. On one occasion she wanted to bring in the black chauffeur to share their meal at a restaurant. The management refused. So she took her meal and shared it with the chauffeur while sitting in the car. The point was made. Then came Australia, another place where she could rely on a thunderous reception. She again fell on stage because her dress was so tight and the heels of her shoes were too high, there were no concessions to her increasingly pain-wracked frame. As a result of heavy smoking her blood vessels were constricted she gave up cigarettes on medical orders, her limbs continued to ache. She drowned the pain with whisky. Another reason why she tottered on stage in Sydney, fell and broke two ribs. But the show went on. After one 50 minute ovation at the Theatre Royal in Sydney she finally had to say, 'Please go home, I'm tired.'

On the Australian tour she met a bisexual writer called Hugh Curnow. He joined her for a walk along the ocean shore and persuaded her to let him help on her biography. After he became her lover she agreed. He returned with her to her Paris flat to work on the book. They went through her scrap books tucked under the bed, then made love upon it with her astride a man 40 years her junior, then returned to her reminiscences. But she did not earn his admiration, he went back to Australia and wrote some devastating articles about her, even complaining that her preferred method of love making did not allow him an active role. It was partly Marlene's preferred method, and it lessened the pain from her cancer treatment when she could control which parts of her he stimulated. Curnow's ruthless appraisal of the aging movie star included a description of unwinding her out of her costume after a show 'like some mummy being unwound'.

At a press reception held at Adelaide Airport Hugh Curnow was decapitated by a helicopter blade. Marlene Dietrich made love to no more men, bad things seemed to happened to them after being with her.

She was still in love with Burt Bacharach, even though he had married Angie Dickinson. In October 1967 she reunited with him for a Broadway season staged by Alexander Cohen who was determined to be the first to persuade Marlene to appear on Broadway. The price of her acceptance was that he hire Burt Bacharach as musical director. He astonished her by pulling the deal off. The New York critics were glowing, 'a dream returned' said the New York Times. Her sense of well being had never been better, the old team was back in town. Rudi was persuaded to come to the opening night party, but he was confused by the theatre crowds and had visibly shrunk with age. In the audience for the opening night was Noel Coward, who remained a devoted friend and adviser on her career.

Marlene's friends and contemporaries were disappearing into death's arms. Some deaths made more impact than others. Jean Cocteau had died the same day as Edith Piaf, that had shaken but not surprised her. Judy Garland went, but she had longed for this escape. Marlene was asked for a comment.

'If you want to die, go die, don't be a bore about it,' she replied.

Few knew as well as her Judy Garland's pain and suffering, it seemed like a welcome release. There were sad memories, of how Judy had befriended Maria in pre-war days, they were two little girls united against the world of Hollywood, but as entranced as anyone by the glamour and the glitz of it all.

In 1969 Josef von Sternberg died. She had always kept up with him, offered him her respect and devotion but had seen how his strange genius had been unable able to find another vehicle after their partnership. They often discussed what were their best films. Marlene was convinced *The Devil is a Woman* had seen portrayed her at her most stunning. The under-rated film had been used as the story line for the launch of Brigitte Bardot in Roger Vadim's *And God Created Woman*. It proved a stunning introduction to her waif-like, free and easy appeal, as powerful for her as Marlene's own appearance as a sex siren under von Sternberg's tutelage. Both knew she was fated to be remembered as The Blue Angel, whatever Josef von Sternberg or she might have preferred. Even *Shanghai Express* could not dislodge the image of the back street singer in the waterfront bars of old Lubeck. Marlene kept original reels of all her films among the thousands of souvenirs of the movie business she amassed - she always collected her nameplate on the dressing room door of a studio production and many of the costumes created for her stayed with her. In 1959, the Museum of Modern Art ran a retrospective on her career where she lent them some of the film original prints, they were final proof of her labours and art, in all the whirlwind tours she made sure they stayed in a safe place. She was convinced one day they would be valued at their true worth with a museum built in Berlin to commemorate the rise of a German star. Her grandson has now negotiated their sale for just such a museum, where Marlene Dietrich waits her final recognition.

But she was not yet ready to be a museum piece. The need to perform, to go out and meet her audience all around the world was as compulsive as ever. And a further challenge still remained. After the success of the New York 'Queen of the World' show, Alex Cohen began a long campaign for her to make a TV spectacular.

It was not until 1972 that the final arrangements for the TV show were made. It was to be shot in London at the newly built New London Theatre, Drury Lane, in the heart of theatreland. The fee was settled at $250,000 for a one-hour performance. She had approval of the proposed set - a luscious pink, the musical arranger - Stan Freeman, who replaced her beloved Burt Bacharach. She also sought to get her way over the lighting and sound. Alex Cohen protested, she reminded him of her apprenticeship under the great von Sternberg, the relationship got more and more difficult the closer they came to the taping of the TV show, to be called *I Wish You Love*, which would go out on New Year's Day in America, followed a week later by the British premiere.

The magic of the live show did not translate well to television, there was none of the intimate rapport with the audience on which she depended. People in the flesh she could weave a spell on, but the TV screen offers a poor substitute for experience, cosiness replaces the raw emotion of humanity which is curiously there in a large cinema audience. She was so disappointed by the finished TV show that it spilled over into a legal battle with Alexander Cohen who described her as the most difficult performer he had ever had to deal with. It took years for the matter to be resolved.

Marlene hated the TV show for its revelations of her increasing world weariness. Although her flesh-coloured body corset gave the illusion of a figure belonging to a forty-year-old, there was less that could be done for her aching limbs, which gave her sharp stabs of pain when they precariously balanced on high heels. The famous legs proved reluctant to take even the few steps onto stage that the precisely worked details of her act demanded. Her last show in English theatres was the next year in 1973, at Wimbledon Theatre, in London's south west suburbs. It is one of the larger old-style music halls surviving from Edwardian times, there are many ghosts inhabiting its precincts and stage. Here, one more time, the legend came on swathed in lights, stood before her audience and received tribute for the seeming defiance of time itself. Her routine varied not all, from *Lilli Marlene* to *The Boys in the Backroom,* finishing with *Falling in Love Again.* The bars fade, *'I give you my love,'* she says simply and quietly, flowers land at her feet from stage right and stage left, the audience rises, they shower each other with gratitude and affection for all the hard times they have come through, the wars, the losses, the heartache. Audience and performer celebrate their survival and it is time to go, she is saddened but unbowed.

Chapter Seventeen

The curtain comes down

In November 1973, when she was giving a show at the Shady Grove Music Fair near Washington, the time came for her to take the ovation once again. She leaned forward in a deep bow and held out her hand to Stan Freeman, her musical director, in the orchestra pit. He was precariously balanced on a stool to reach her and began to wobble just as he held her hand. They tumbled into the pit together, her dress was ripped revealing her foundation garment.

'Bring a blanket to cover me, don't move me,' she ordered the startled ushers who came rushing over.

Only when the theatre had been cleared would she allow myself to be carried out. At first it seemed there was just a long deep cut in her thigh, nothing, surprisingly, had been broken. But overnight the wound turned ugly. She rang Senator Edward Kennedy to find out the name of his doctor. He was waiting at a hospital for his nephew's leg to be amputated and did not take the call. Finally, she booked into a private clinic in New York, where they decided she needed a skin graft. The poor supply of blood to her legs from constricted veins meant the wound was not healing, while the skin graft turned out to be both a long and painful procedure which kept her bedbound for nearly four months. It did not, however, prevent her from making a scheduled appearance at London's Grosvenor House Hotel on Park Lane in 1974. Marlene was wheeled to the edge of the stage and then took careful steps in front of the audience to thunderous applause. The press were kept well away, although Princess Margaret came to see her in her dressing room.

Marlene Dietrich's fragile bones were threatening to end her stage career, she fell in Paris and broke a hip. But the worst break of all was yet to come. In 1974 in Sydney she was about to play to a half empty house, when she felt her leg give way beneath her just as she walked on stage. She fell very awkwardly, so awkwardly that she broke her leg, with the femur bone in the thigh piercing through the skin. Ginette Vachon, a wealthy Canadian who had become a friend, cradled Marlene in her arms on the way to hospital after she had been carried in a fireman's lift to the dressing room by the burly stage manager. Maria and Ginette put into effect the booking for her flight from Australia. To keep away prying eyes they booked her in the first class section, where eight seats were curtained off from the rest of the passengers. Elaborate precautions were made to prevent her being photographed when they landed at Los Angeles International Airport. She was swept off to the UCLA Medical Centre where Rudi was also in the hospital. He had suffered a serious stroke at the chicken farm and his life hung in the balance while Marlene lay in a bed next door to him, her leg encased in plaster. After three days she was transferred to New York's Columbia-Presbyterian Medical Center under the name of Sieber and there she lay for more long months, aware that her stage career was over.

Rudi died some time later on June 24, 1976 without Marlene at his side, she had only been recently released from hospital. He was buried in the graveyard behind Paramount studio, a 100 yards from Tamara. He was 79. With the light of her life extinguished she felt no need to return to the stage, her inspiration was gone. She returned to her apartment in Paris and contemplated how she would earn a living. By a quirk of fate her leg fracture had occurred four days before an insurance policy on her legs issued by Lloyds of London expired, but for a woman who had been earning at least a million dollars a year ever since the 1960s from her shows, the sudden cessation of income was a drastic development. There were some receipts from records, popular still in Germany and France, she dallied with writing her biography, which was eventually published by Bertelsmann in Germany. Some jewels were sold, then a film offer came through from Germany. The offer was to play Baroness von Semering in a film entitled in English *Just a Gigolo* which featured the singer David Bowie. Directed by David Hemmings, who had played the photographer in Antonioni's *Blow Up*, it offered her a small cameo part as the keeper of a house of gigolos in the decadent days of Berlin after the First World War.

Part of the contract was that the film crew would come to Paris for the shots of her singing to gigolo Paul von Przygodsky (David Bowie), as he sits at Berlin's Eden Bar. The reason he is not shown in the same frame as Marlene is because he had finished his film work and was in the Caribbean by the time the crew moved to Paris for her two short scenes. David Hemmings helped her overcome her film set nerves with a steadying large glass of whisky, even though it was early in the morning. She had to sing an old Berlin song about being *Just a Gigolo* to the doomed Bowie, who afterwards wanders out of the bar and is shot in a street fight between the Nazis and the Communists.

For this part as the Baroness she made herself up as the Marlene of legend, but it did not please Hemmings, who sent her to be made up again by Anthony Clavet. He produced a startling transformation, here was a new Marlene, older, veiled, mysterious, ineffably sad and weary, but still capable of hinting at the allure of female beauty. She walked on set, held her head at the correct angle for the overhead lights and began to sing in a throaty rich voice a song that had been a hit on Berlin's streets when she was hardly more than a girl.

The words had a poignancy for Marlene.

'People pay, you keep on dancing.'
'There will come a day
When love will fade away

What will people say?
Just a gigolo
Life goes on without me.'

David Hemmings watched spellbound as all the aches of the years were poured into those lines. He was unable to call out 'Cut' till long after the take was in the can. Marlene walked off the set, some $25,000 richer, her film career at an end. It was not a bad way to go, remembering where it had all begun, in Germany's most expensive post-war production, partly financed by the Berlin Senate. She had almost come home.

But there was another film tribute to come. An inspired documentary from the Austrian actor Maximillian Schell who took up a project that Maria had been trying to sell to the film studios in order to raise some much needed cash for both mother and daughter. In 1982 Maximillian began four days of questioning using a tape recorder. The old Hollywood star refused to be photographed for the film, or even to allow the cameras in her Paris apartment. It is a measure of Maximilian's artistic ingenuity that he was able to construct out of this unlikely setting a masterful film which intersperses many of Marlene's favourite film clips with his remorseless questioning of her. She told him the films were just work. That it was others who romanticised and sentimentalised her. That Lola Lola had no appeal for her, that Orson Welles was a genius whose name should only be mentioned with reverence. Still Schell kept on probing. The fact she had a sister who was still alive came out. True, but Marlene had cut Elisabeth out of her thoughts after her sister's and her husband's links with Belsen concentration camp became clear, even if they were only running a cinema for officers in the town and had little to do with the actual running of the extermination camp. Schell probed about her father. He even knew her mother's favourite poem, linked to her father, Schell persuaded her to recite it and Marlene broke down in tears as the long distant memories of her dear Papa came flooding back in her 82nd year, some 75 years since she had last seen him. The Austrian actor turned director knew enough about Marlene to be able to get under the skin, he realised more than most that the Marlene of the films was a mask and a protection, and because he was such a good actor she respected him, revealing more than she intended. The drinks flowed, she did not know the crew were recording as the conversation continued after a day's work. Maximilian Schell captured her more fully than anyone else who had interviewed her, but only after he had walked out saying that there was no contract unless she did it his way. The next day the fury and bombast had subsided, Marlene signed. The project was designed to finance her and Maria's family through her last years, she had little choice but to give in.

Money had flowed through her hands all her life. More jewellery was sold at Christie's in 1987. The landlords were paid off by Paris City Council after they threatened to evict her for non-payment of her rent. It meant something to the town authorities that she carried one of France's highest honours. The dreadful Bertlesmann biography written in English, translated into German, translated into French, translated back into English, was finally in the shops by the end of the 1980s but it hid more than it revealed, Marlene was not going to kiss and tell like the new breed of actresses.

In her last years she became an icon for the rehabilitation of Germany. The press rang her for her reaction when the Berlin wall came down. The Berlin papers rang again when they wanted her to support the campaign to save *Neubabelsburg* when the original UFA studios were threatened in 1991. A sound stage was named after her there.

Life continued outside her flat, but Marlene hardly left her bed, still less the building. Books and letters poured in from round the world, she read, drank, read some more, kept in touch with old friends on the telephone and if they were ever in town, refused to see them. Billy Wilder tried to look her up and she told him Miss Dietrich was out of town, claiming to be the maid, he was not fooled but eventually gave up trying. The person they sought no longer existed, the old Marlene lay preserved in her film masters, press clippings and fading mementoes. The private Maria Magdalene Dietrich was alone with her memories and her poets, Heine and Rilke, Goethe and Schiller. On the phone she would talk to any old friends and reflect on 90 years of living. Towards the end of April 1992, she felt herself ebbing away, very slowly, the beat of life in her cells losing its warm glow. She rang Michael Thornton, a graduate of King's College London, who had long been a confidante since he had interviewed her for his college newspaper.

'I'm going now,' she hoarsely whispered to him.

Then there was silence. The long tumult of the century had come to an end.

Thank you for reading The Blue Angel *I hope you have enjoyed reading it as much I enjoyed researching the story of Marlene Dietrich, and a special message of thanks to Bernhard Hall her assistant in her later years who gave me some wonderful insights into the lady.*

David Stuart Ryan

David Stuart Ryan

For more details of books from Kozmik Press and David Stuart Ryan visit our website

www.kozmikhoroscopes.com/kozmik.htm

Printed in Great Britain
by Amazon

44265149R00109